The Long Journey

Second Edition

James L. Bryant, Jr.

Copyright © 2018, 2008 by James L. Bryant, Jr.

All rights reserved. No part of this publication may be reproduced, distributed, or transmitted in any form or by any means, including photocopying, recording, or other electronic or mechanical methods, without the prior written permission of the author, except in the case of brief quotations embodied in critical reviews and certain other noncommercial uses permitted by copyright law.

Printed in the United States of America

ISBN: Paperback: 978-1-948172-77-6
        eBook: 978-1-948172-76-9

Library of Congress Control Number: 2018945890

 STONEWALL PRESS
PAVING YOUR WAY TO SUCCESS

Stonewall Press
363 Paladium Court
Owings Mills, MD 21117
www.stonewallpress.com
1-888-334-0980

Contents

Introduction v

Chapter One 1
Chapter Two 17
Chapter Three 33
Chapter Four 49
Chapter Five 67
Chapter Six 83
Chapter Seven 99
Chapter Eight 117
Chapter Nine 135
Chapter Ten 153
Chapter Eleven 171

Introduction

Characters: mother and father, sister and brothers, grandmother, grandfather, cousins, uncles and aunts, friends, churches and schools, personal thoughts on the world's problems, outlook for the future and experience on my life's journey, spiritual blessings and problems with our public officials.

Chapter One

It all started in Mississippi, a small town, named Wesson, Mississippi, born on a small farm to a share cropper. My Father was named James Bryant sr., and mother name was Flora Bryant. Both were living in the same county and knew one another all off their young lives. My life as I know it started at age 4 or 5; this was the approximate age that I developed an urge to write something.

    The old farm house that we lived in belong to a plantation owner, all the land that my father plowed and farmed belonged to the same plantation owner. The crops that father planted, half were given to the plantation owner, some times the crops did not do well, but father still had to give half of his crops to the owner. The winters were especially hard, we gathered all the remains of the crops and mother canned them for winter, some of the crops; corn, beans, potatoes, peas, peaches, tomatoes. We had other vegetables in my mother's garden. Most farm products were eaten on a daily basis.

    Church/School; we went to school at the same place that we attended church. There was one big room for all grades, the same room that we had our church services in, the grades extended from 1st, through 6. Church service was every Sunday, from early in the morning to late in the evening. Each family had to bring food; there were many chickens, cakes, vegetables, and other foods. For young children, this was the ideal thing, good food, cousins, and friends. The thing that the children feared most, was the" Grave Yard" directly in the back of the Church House. The old grave stones, some were only marked by a big rock or stone, what ever they could use to identify a grave. Many times I wondered, who were those old graves, who did they belong to, were they old slaves that had passed on or how did they die? They could have been soldiers who had fought in the civil war, or some of the Indian wars. Many were probably slaves buried in the woods.

Father working in the woods; when the weather was too wet to plow the fields, Father, uncle Henry and two cousins, would go to the woods to cut paper wood. They had an old ford flat bed truck with high stakes on each corner of the bed to keep the logs from rolling off; they also had a flat bed Chevy that was rigged the same way. They carried their lunches, 3 or 4 different saws for cutting down the timber. They used a two man saw, one pulled and the other pushed, they did this repeatedly, until the tree had been fallen, then they would trim off all of the limbs and loaded them on the trucks. Some times, the ground was so muddy that mud was up to the axle of the trucks, those old trucks came out of the woods fully loaded, coming out in a double low gear. They always seem to come out and get to the saw mill. On the way back, they would stop at the old grocery store. They would purchase candy and soda pops for us. Sometime we would go and visit our grandparent's home. We had many cousins that would come from all around the county area to be together on the farm. There were some that came up from Chicago to have a family reunification, we all enjoyed farm life and relatives, just being together and having fun. We would run through the pasture, teasing the animals on the farm we would all meet down on grandfather's farm, 3 or 4 miles from where we lived on a share cropper's property. One long graveled road, with tall trees on each side of the road, dark in the evening and pit dark at night. Only lights we had were kerosene lamps. We would sit on the front porch of my grandfather's house and watch the stars go by, making wishes, and wondering what was up there. Lighting bugs would fly about and we would snatch them out off the air, using the pretty colored bugs as rings around our fingers if though we had a gold ring.

In the mornings, grandfather would arise early; feed the farm animals; chickens, hogs, cattle and other farm animals, mules and horses. He would get the working animals together to be ready for a day's work plowing his fields. Children gathered stove wood for grandmother, and grandfather had the mules rigged for plowing the fields. After he had been there in the fields plowing for a few hours, grandmother would send two off us down to tell grandfather to come and eat breakfast. The aroma, the smell of food cooking filled the clean, clear early morning air, the smell of fresh brewed coffee, smell of bacon or ham was in the air, fresh biscuits cooking. Even the birds were singing. Animals of all kind would be out and about, during what nature had intended for them to do. Snakes would some times cross our paths. We would bring the mules back to the barn to be fed and watered when we left the field for breakfast or lunch. Table was set; we all sat down to enjoy a wonderful breakfast. After every one had blessing over the food, we began to eat. We talked about many things, what we wanted to be in life, what was our out look for the future. We all had our dreams and each person's dream was applauded, grandfather would then say what he thought and his aspirations. We took about two hours for breakfast.

Back to the fields to plow the mules and breaking new ground. Uncle Emanuel, mother's oldest brother, who lived on part of the farm, helped grandfather with plowing; he had his own family to provide for. This was a family affair. When the fields were plowed, the crops planted, we went fishing and played games. Daily chores continued, feeding the farm animals, gathering fire wood, cleaning the barn etc. One day three off the cousins went fishing down to the big pond, grandfather had two water ponds on his many acres of land, for cattle and horses to drink water, and the little pond was farther out into the pasture. The big pond was near the lot or corral, not very far from the farm house. It was hot on this day, we took bamboo polls as fishing poles and many night crawlers to catch cat fish, as we were walking around the perimeter of the pond, there were large willow trees hanging over the pond, these trees offered shade to many animals from the hot sun. We were walking in a single file, one behind another. Suddenly, there was a huge" water moccasin snake" hanging from a limb over looking the pond in our pathway, swinging back and forth. I called out, "snake that's on the over hanging limb", I quickly made an about face, and started to run back in the direction that we had come, nearly running over the other cousins. We arrived back at the farm house and told grandfather what we had seen, grandfather immediately, grabbed his 20 gauge shotgun and went back down to the pond where we pointed the snake out to grandfather. When he fired the 20 gage shot gun, limbs, snake and any thing else that was near the snake fell into the pond. Our fishing trip ended for that day. We found other things to do. We went down to the watermelon patch and plucked a few of grandfather's watermelons.

Cotton fields, very hot and dry, I hated the "cotton fields" more than I did any other crop that we had to harvest. There were snakes, huge horned worms and other insects. Bailing hay and cutting sugar cane. We had many crops to harvest, grandmother and the other women would can fruits, and vegetables, putting things away for a rainy day. When all chores were completed, the products were divided up between all of his children. Time was about up for my great vacation, it seems to come too soon, it was time to go back home and prepare to go to school and to help my father with his chores. Back to the old school house that sat on a hill with one big room to have church services. We shared the same building for both, school and church, walking to and back from school, having fun in doing it, watching strange animals cross our path. This was the same long, narrow road that grandfather and other relatives lived on. I remember the old grocery store at the fork of the road; this is where we bought things that we needed to fill in the short comings; salt, flour sugar, kerosene and other odds and ends. Occasionally, there would be a grocery store coming by on wheels, selling 25 to 50 lbs., of ice. When we purchased ice we would make fresh ice cream, this was a good time, I had the experience of making ice cream with an old hand cranked, ice cream maker, you churned and churned away until the cream, and other mixtures were blended together, the ice froze the mixtures and made ice cream.

From Wesson to Jackson, Mississippi, this was a time of truth for me, leaving the only place that I knew and going to a foreign big city. Father finally, left Wesson, and he arrived in Jackson, where he had sisters and brothers living. At the request of his older brother and sister, he left the farm and settled in Jackson. He found a job at the contractors' material company; this was a steel factory which was hot and sweaty work. He was up to the task; he had worked even harder on the farm. The money was more than he had ever earned before. We moved to a house on sidway near mill Street this is a major street that run from north to south with a heavy flow of traffic, we were becoming more comfortable with our surroundings, locating the nearest grocery store and play grounds, begun to make friends. School was not far from where we lived. Smith Robertson, the name of the school that I went to was all Black, all Black Teachers, janitors, and other public workers. I was in the third grade when I attended school in Jackson. Un-like on the farm, I had more time to play and enjoy the new friends that I had made. We done our home work and we had time to play, we explored our neighborhood, we knew who lived where, and all the kids that were there. Later, we wanted to earn money, we wanted to go to the movies. On Saturdays, we went to the movies and made a whole day of it. The most popular were; westerns, jungle Jim, distant drum and others. Sundays, we went to Sunday school and stayed there for regular church services.

Making money; there were many ways that we could make some money, it was not very much, it supplied our needs, we mowed lawns, raked leaves, and other yard maintenance. We hunted cock roaches at night. Using flash lights, we waited until dark and the cock roaches would come out around the garbage cans and other places where they could find food. Where you find one or two usually, you would find five or six in one place. We would go from house to house, calling out "roach boy, when residents heard you say" roach boy", they would feel relieved, knowing that we were not burglars. We would receive 1or2 cents per cock roach; some times we would catch 2to3 hundred roaches per person per night. Some time we would sell the cock roaches to workers that worked at the train station, other times fishermen would come by to buy all that we had. We earned two or three dollars a night for each person. After being settled in our new surroundings, we prepared to go back to grandfather's farm. We had to help grandfather with his crops. Cousins were coming from Chicago to spend a few weeks of summer on the farm to help with the chores. This was good news, to hear that all of the relatives were coming down for the summer. We have the coming together of the Elias Hayes, clan. There were two sons and four daughters in his family. Grandmother's sister lived directly behind grandfather's farm, about a mile traveling through the forest; this was a scary experience, going to visit cousins on the hill. We had to travel on a narrow path that had many over hanging trees, we had to be careful of snakes and other unknowns that we might encounter, after reaching our destination, and we played games and ate fruit and tea cookies. After many hours of playing and enjoying one's company, we started the trip back to grandfather's farm, this time we had another cousin to come with us. We took the short cut back home. We were in no hurry to get back. We played games and picked wild plums, on our way back home, we had to go over or crawl under a barbed wire fence to get back to the farm house. There were mean bulls and two young mules that didn't like intrusions; the animals would start chasing us.

We had to be fast to get back over or under the barbed wire fence. When reaching the other side we began to tease the mules and bulls. In reaching the farm house, we sat on the front porch to catch our breath. The other cousin that came back with us, nick named ;" Sugar man" we gave him this name because he ate so much sugar cane. Nearly any thing that we could be involved in, we were involved in, from killing snakes to teasing some off the farm animals. We picked wild plums, nuts, peaches and pears. We took watermelons from grandfather's watermelon patch; we cut a one inch square on the top of the melon to see which one was ripe and ready for us to eat. When asked about the melons that had been eaten, we lied to him about it. Grandfather didn't take it too kindly that we would lie.

Grandfather's new tractor was something new on the farm, a big green in color, John Deer tractor, he never would use it. He would keep it clean and shinny, stored away in the huge shop shed. He probably, didn't know how to operate it, or he had more confidence in horses and mules to do his farm work. However, he did buy a tractor and kept it in superb condition. My first feel at a plow was given to me by a first cousin; he was the oldest of all the males' cousins on the Hayes side of the family. Mother's oldest brother's son, we called him Emanuel his true name. He took me and other cousins down to the field to break up new ground, each cousin would take turns in trying to steady the mule and keep straight lines plowing, it was not as easy as we thought it would be. Directing the mule to respond to your command, what to say to the mule to go left or to the right. To keep straight or stop, slow down or speed up. It was truly a unified effort between mule and master. It took me a while to understand why farmers loved their farming animals so much, without them you could hardly do any farming. .Animals Were well fed and cared for. Time was coming fast for us to think about returning to our homes, we had a few weeks to go before we would be packing for home. Some were from Illinois, and some were from other towns in Mississippi. During most summers, we would meet and come together at grandfather's farm. On Sundays, traditionally, we all went to Church, as before, we took the whole day to stay at church, there were foods of all kind, each family donated cooked food of their choice, we enjoyed the services and the food.

Most Families arrived at church in wagons pulled by two horses or mules. When the feast was over, we prayed Blessings to see us safely home and through out the week. A trip to the grocery store would occur, things were written down on brown paper to bring back. Ice was one of the main items to bring back. The wagon and horses or mules was hooked up, we set out to the grocery store, making a few stops along the way. Asking some others along the way if they needed anything special from the store, if so, we waited until they wrote down on brown paper what they needed for us to bring back for them. All items they asked for were purchased. Stops back along the way was keep at a minimum, we had to get back home before the ice melted under the hot Mississippi sun. The ice was covered with gunny sacks to keep the melt at a minimum. We arrived, and began to unload the groceries and ice, we put the ice in the old ice box, saving it to make ice cream and we had enough people to take turns in churning the ice cream machine. Ice cream would be made later in the week, usually, on Saturdays.

All of the Hayes arrived early on Saturday morning; they came to spend a day or two with other sisters and brothers. My mother and father, James and Flora Bryant, came down from Jackson, Aunt Oral Mae and her husband, J.N. Brooks Came down from Chicago to join the family reunion; it was a great time together. Aunt Blanchard and her family came down to the farm from another county in Mississippi. Games were played, stories were told and good food was served.

Ticket to have a chance to win a new car, Grandfather was lucky and won a new car. There were many angry white people, they could not understand, black man buys one new car and wins another, all on the same day. This was never heard off, they wanted to know where he got the money to purchase the new car, and now he ends up winning a second one. He could not leave the dealer ship with both new cars, he had to let one of his white farmer friends drive the new car to his home and hide it in his barn. Grandfather knew he would be visited by the racist .whites. In spite of all the injustices on Black people in this racist State, you still could find a few Whites that would try to help you. Grandfather had to sell the new car that he had won to the same person that drove the car from the dealer ship. Stories and conversations continued until night. We sat on the front porch to watch the moon and the stars, it was a beautiful hot night, cousins tried to snatch lighting bugs from the sky, using the gold lighted bugs to place around our fingers, pretending to have a gold ring. We had to get all of our belongings together to prepare to leave the farm and back to our homes. Early, on Sunday morning we would be leaving.

The Long Journey

We came together, we prayed, some farm produce were distributed. There were nuts, peaches, corn, potatoes and a few more things that we took back to Jackson. Aunt Oral and family left to go back to Chicago. Aunt Blanche and family went back to their home in Brookhaven, Mississippi, Uncle Emanuel was already at home, he lived on the property only a mile away. Father had purchased a 48 or 49 fleet wood Chevy, grey in color, large enough to carry six people and all of the luggage and farm produce that we carried back with us. The front seat was for my mother and sister, father was the driver. Three boys, all brothers was sitting in the back, We had much fun, talking about our experience on the farm, talking about cousins, uncles and aunts, being glad to see and be with some of the cousins that we did not see very often. We stopped along the highway a few times before arriving in Jackson, enjoying the scenery, the farms and animals. The distance from Wesson is about forty-five minutes drive or about forty miles to Jackson; we got home safely and we began to unload the old Chevy, things were taken into the house and the brothers immediately, began to look for our friends, to let them know that we were back in town. We hated to leave the farm, leaving our cousins and grandparents, leaving all the farm animals behind, but we knew we had made friends in Jackson before we had left. Those same friends would be friends forever. The first year in Jackson we had proven that you can conquer your surroundings. I was the oldest of the three boys, my sister was the oldest child, and her name is Florene. James, Eli, and Samuel who is the youngest of the clan Eli was the brave one of the boys, there were nothing that he was afraid off, he loved animals, all kinds, dogs were his favorite animal. Brother Eli, took sick and was diagnosed as a diabetic, it just didn't seem right for a young boy with love for every thing had such illness. He suffered terribly, having to take insulin, having a strict diet, limitations on activity and stress. However, he was able to go to our friend's home on Saturday night, to watch Big time wrestling and some Friday night boxing. Our best friends were all ways together on those two nights. The" Banjo brother's" home were where we mostly went to on Saturday nights, and most Friday nights, we would come together to watch these events. They had a large house and a large family, four boys and three girls, their mother would cook pop corn in a huge pot so there would be enough for all. Other close friends were Edward lee Green, my next door neighbor, George E. Day, Alfonso Benjamin, Charles Anthony. These were the best of friends, we done mostly, everything together, hunting for cock roaches at night, mowing lawns, raking leaves and other chores.

Going back to school; all good things must come to an end. Back to school and meet more friends. This time, we had to register at another school, the old Smith Robertson School was being renovated and grades one through eight had to go to the new school. I thought that this was a good school not being far from where I lived, only a few blocks away. Rowan was the name of the school. It was a beautiful school with better class rooms and cafeteria. I participated in sports, baseball, basketball; football and all sport that I tried out for except, swimming, basketball seem to be my favorite sport. We had to play a school they call the "deaf and dumb", the kids were rough players, they would foul you hard and the referee acted if he saw nothing, he would let the game continue without interruption. There were football, which was worst, we had to play the same "deaf and dumb" school that we had played in basketball, it seems they had a score to settle and we would be the one they would settle it with, or they wanted to prove to coaches and fans that they were as good or better than we were. We sometimes stayed after school and played basketball on the out doors court, there were no concrete or paved court on the outside, and it was made hard by constant playing on the hard surface. There was no way they would allow us to play in the gym, which was reserved for school activity. My sister went to another school, when they closed down Smith Robertson, she went to Lanier High School, she had to walk across Mill Street which was a very busy street and then across the rail road yard which had many tracks to cross, the school was about a mile from where we lived. Sometime we were told to meet her and walk her back home. She eventually, met a young man by the name of Arthur Spires, who attended the same school and who lived on the west side of the tracks, he would sometimes walk her home. He Introduced him self to the family. It took a few introductions, to convince the family that he was to be trusted. Later, the family began

The Long Journey

to like him and placed a little more trust in him, and then he began to seem to be potentially, part off the family. The walking and courting continued, soon they would be going on dates, mostly to the movies on Saturdays. My brother, Eli, and myself, had to go along with them, we sat in the front of the theater and they would sit in the back, a few rows in the rear of us. We enjoyed ourselves, eating popcorn, hot dogs and ice cream. We saw westerns, jungle movies, ghost stories and other movies. Distant drum was one of my favorite, gone with the wind, rising in the sun, all good for watching. When movies was over, we began the long walk back home, brothers went in side of the house and let her and friend say good bye to each other.

Sundays; we went to church, attended Sunday school and stayed for regular services. Strangers home Baptist Church. This was an all brick building that had about one hundred members.

There were good church programs. After church, we would just hang out and prepare for school the next day. During the fall months, things began to slow down; the way we earned money was coming to a slow pace, we raked leaves, hunted cock roaches and other odd jobs. Not far from where we lived, there was a café, we could go there and buy hot link sausages and pig ear sandwiches, you could buy soft drinks of all flavors, such as root beer, coca cola, royal crown cola and other flavors. We played the pin ball machine, shot pool. You could play with a penny or five cents. You could win one hundred and twenty penny or nickels if you could put three, four, or five steel balls in the holes that were embedded into the table. Many times we played and lost, sometimes we won. We had to figure out a way to win more; we had to divide the winnings up among four or five people. Some one made a suggestion of how we could make the machine pay off more, and more frequently, we had one lucky person to shoot the steel balls into the holes, if he could not make all five holes, then we all would stand behind the machine and along the sides. This was to obstruct the vision of any one seeing what we were doing. A coat hanger had been straightened out and bent on the end; the hanger was used to light up the pockets that we needed to win. The scheme worked, we

11

made money each time we went in there to play. Owner began to get curious; he knew it was not possible that any one could win that often. One day, he figured out what was going on. He then asked us to leave; we did and left the café in a hurry. If we expected to receive any thing for Christmas, we had to be on our best behavior, be smart, obedient and stay out of trouble. All received gifts for Christmas; some got new bicycle, scooter, wagon, and other toys. We had fruits and nuts, candies and a shirt or blue jeans. This truly, the best holiday of the year, a short time to be out of school to enjoy Christmas and all the gifts that came with it. What ever we received we were thankful and tried to preserve them, knowing that what we had received did not come easy, father and mother had to work hard to get the things for Christmas that we had received. All the friends made their rounds to one another to show off their new toys. Samuel, youngest brother received a big red wagon, Eli the second youngest, received a two wheel scooter with back foot brakes, and I received a road master bicycle, it had white wall tires and a basket on it and luggage carrier over the rear wheel. Two weeks of enjoying Christmas, was hard to go back to school. Samuel was still too young to be at school so mother stayed home to take care of him until he became of age to go to school. Mother took in domestic work at home, she would wash and iron clothes for some of the white doctors, and lawyers, she made extra money to help father pay the bills. After staying home for a year or so, Samuel, was ready for school, after he was in school, mother began to work out side of the home, and she would work a few hours of the day. She had children to raise and a husband to look after and feed, father was still working at the steel mill and he left work about three o'clock pm. We all wanted to get home before father did, when he arrived, we all were there. Mother had already, started dinner, and sister was helping her. We used gas for cooking and heating in Jackson, unlike on the farm where all had to help with wood. On the week end, especially, Friday, Saturday was the time father used to unwind after a hard week's work, brothers coming together to relieve stress. These are the names of relatives on my father's side of the family, he came from a family of twenty four sisters and brothers, and they were a close family that enjoyed one another company. Sonny, the oldest brother, Rosetta , second oldest,

The Long Journey

Green, third oldest, Laura, Henry, Jessie Bell, John c, Lu La, these are a few of the sisters and brothers, only the ones that lived close to where we lived, some lived in other towns in Mississippi and other States.

Fred, Robert, John lee, these were nephews of my father, aunt Laura's, children, there were more but these were the closet ones to where we lived in Jackson, on Saturday, they came together to celebrate a hard work week they some time went hunting, and went fishing. They enjoyed being together, uncles and nephews.

My father was the hardest working man that you would ever see, he loved his family and would do any thing for us, and he always worked, making a living for his family. The next summer it would not be an enjoyable summer for the children, we had to go to the delta, we went there to pick cotton, the terrain was huge, miles of cotton fields, hot and dry, dusty, snakes, horned worms striped like a zebra, you had to be careful where you put your hands. I saw mother and father along with other cotton pickers, drag sacks that would hold a hundred pounds of cotton; we helped mother and father fill their cotton sacks. When the sacks were filled, he needed help in dragging the sacks to the weigh station. You always had less cotton in the sack than what you thought that you had. Cotton was weighed with a pea scale. There was an over seer that was white. There could have been some cheating going on. We worked in the cotton fields for four or five weeks. On the week end, we would go to a movie or just hang around. The old shacks, built for slaves or share croppers, shaggy and run down, pump your water and get by the best way that we could. These were horrible conditions for any one to have to live in, regardless of how long we would be there. There were no stores, only a shed that carried few things and it was owned by the plantation owner, you would get paid for your hard work and gave the money back to him in purchasing of his merchandise, I saw this as being a no win situation. Returning back to Jackson; all of the people came on the converted bus with us, began to load all of their belongings on the bus for the trip back to Jackson. Glad to leave this God forsaken place, I had experienced a terrible ordeal in the delta. I thought of suffering a heat exhaustion, I had drunk too much ice water; I was so thirsty, the more I drank the more thirsty I became. Mother and father laid me under a big shady oak tree and stayed by my side until I recovered, it took two hours before I could recover.

The delta was in northwest, Mississippi and about a four-hour drive, there were stops along the way, the country side looked different than what I was use to seeing, not very much green vegetation.

Seemed to be warmer than Jackson, this was the last stop before reaching home, this was good, maybe we could reunite with our friends. The only thing that I learned from the trip was to never go back there again. We arrived in Jackson, made stops; dropped people off at certain stops then proceeded to come home.

We arrived, and began to unload our belongings .Mother gave thanks to God for arriving safely home. We arrived on Saturday, the same day that we had left the delta, we cleaned up and rested for a few hours, then mother began to prepare for dinner. The boys were ready for action, we wanted to locate our friends and have fun, and we wanted to tell friends about our trip. Friends were found and the fun began from that point. We shot marbles, threw pennies to the line that was drawn on the ground, when it was too warm to be in the sun, we played marbles under the house. Those houses sat two to three feet above the ground and it was a perfect place to keep cool and out of the sun. Swimming, sometimes we would go down to the nearest water hole, this particular place was called "blue hole", it seem if though all the animals and snakes knew where to come on a hot day, all had to share the water hole, we had to be careful of the snakes that liked to swim and cool off also, especially, the water moccasins and eels. We knew that it would be dangerous and we had to be careful of broken glass that was at the bottom of the water hole, if we saw any snakes, we ran them out of the water, sometime we missed one and was afraid, and then we tried to beat the snake out of the water. Dinner was served, after meal dishes had to be washed, two oldest boys had to help sister in washing dishes, one of us would wash dishes and the other one would rinse and dry them off. The boys had to help sister in cleaning up the kitchen. Youngest brother didn't have any chores at that time; he was too young to understand the kitchen. However, mother would have him to use a yard broom to sweep leaves and other debris from the front porch and the front yard. After finishing our chores, we were allowed to go and play for a few hours, when time was up mother, or sister would call out for us to come home. Preparing for Sunday school and church services on Sunday, Monday, ready for school this was a new school term and we were anxious to meet new faces and to see old students, not too much had changed from one school term to the other. Moved up one more grade level, there were new students that we had to get to know, where they lived and who were their parents. New students and old students seem to get along just fine. Like all schools, there are students who wanted to be the school house bully. Few wanted to become the king of the hill. There were strict discipline in the school and on the school ground, if by some reason you were not in school during the school hours, you could be picked up by the police or the school security and they brought you back to school. Your parents were contacted, and if they had no knowledge of you being out of school, you would have to sit in the principal's office until school was out. It would be for other students to see you sitting in the principal's office; they knew that you had to have done something wrong; each day there would be one or two students sitting in the office for various reasons. Bell rang for school to let out and students went their own way. I had chores that I had to do most of the time, but after that I was free for a few hours to play. We had fun playing sports; we liked school organized sports, such as basketball, football, baseball and track.

Spring was coming; we had to rake leaves and other debris from the front and back yards. There were construction going on near where we lived and there were tar paper scattered around, and un-used small tar cans around, there was a fire that had been started by the construction workers to get rid of the waste that were generated from the construction.

Brother Eli, "dare devil", found a can of un-used tar and threw it into the fire, the can exploded and all three of the boys got burned, I took the worse hit, Samuel got the next worse burn, Eli, who received the least of the burns. I was burned so badly, that the doctors had to treat me for three weeks, and then bandage my face completely with wrapping gauze; I looked like something out of a horror movie. I was out of school for nearly a month. Two brothers were doing well; they only had to go to the doctor only once. I still have scars on me to this date, but all the color has come back. The injury offered no effects on me mentally or any other way. In returning back to school, I was greeted by students and teachers alike, I was glad to be back and they expressed that they were glad to see me. There were a few things that I had to catch up on in my class room studies, but I caught up with the rest of the class and graduated with the class. Sister, and her boy friend were getting serious, they both, had passed their classes and went to a higher grade, Arthur, was two grades ahead of sister, another year he would be graduating from high school. The family went back to grandfather's farm to spend a few weeks with grandmother and grandfather, back to see cousins and other relatives. Father and mother drove us down to the farm, there mother could re-unite with her twin sister and other family members. Mother and father only could stay there for a couple of days, father had to get back to work in Jackson for Monday morning, and mother had no real commitment to a job. But she went back with father on Sunday to Jackson.

All the cousins came together and talked of their school year. We all wanted to hear from our cousins from Chicago, they always had something of interest to talk about. Then we, the Bryant's family would tell of some of the things that they encountered during the school year. I was asked about my health, and what happened during the tar explosion, how did it happen and just how badly I was burned, how badly Eli and Samuel, my younger Brothers were burned? They were interested in the answers that we gave. Relatives listen and looked on with astonishment and thankfulness.

Chapter Two

After each cousin gave their experiences of the school year, we began to find things to do. We played soft ball, there was a large area in the front of the house, and nearly a fourth of a mile from the house to the gravel road, you could hit the ball as far as you could and it would never reach the gravel road. The best time to play ball was early Saturday mornings. Spectators; mothers fathers, grandparents, and cousins were our fans; eldest of the cousins were the hardest hitters and the best players. Fun was over, and each was given a chore to do, some had to feed live stock and some drew water from the cistern, some of us gathered stove wood from the wood pile. There were no electricity and all of the kerosene lamps had to be filled. There were many cousins that came to visit us. We slept on the floor; there were some that went over to uncle Emanuel's house to spend the night.

Sunday morning; we arose and had a good breakfast, this Sunday, we did not go to church, and we stayed home and rested up after having a long day on Saturday. After breakfast, mother and father loaded their car to go back to Jackson, aunt Oral and her husband were going back to Chicago, aunt Blanche left for home in Brookhaven, Mississippi, about twenty miles away, uncle Emanuel was at home on the farm. Aunt Alberta lived on the farm in the house that grandfather and grandmother lived in, she was the youngest of the Hayes clan. There had been another brother that had passed away. He had lived in Chicago for a few years before he took sick and returned to the farm, Samuel, the second oldest of the children died at home after a long illness, he was a teenager when he passed. I only heard talks about him through mother.

Mondays helping grandfather and grandmother with the chores, we grinded corn, picked corn, cut sugar cane, watered the garden and fed the chickens. Grandfather used his mules to plow new ground. There was much that we could do to help on the farm. This was a far cry from being in the delta. I enjoyed the farm; there were much to do and to see. Once a week or more, the grocery man would come by the farm on wheels, an old truck that was loaded with things of interest; ice, flour, flavors and other merchandise. We purchased one hundred pounds of ice and vanilla abstract for making ice cream. The ice was put in the old ice box for keeping, until ready to make ice cream, Saturdays the time to freeze ice cream. Until that day arrives, we continue to do our chores and to help with what ever was needed; granddaughters would help grandmother with chores around the house. Sister, and other females, helped to cook dinner, prepare supper. Two of the boys would go down to the field where grandfather was plowing and told him that grandmother said for him to come home and eat dinner, we would help grandfather to un-hook the plow and other from the mules and ride them back to the lot to be fed and to give them water, we fed them corn on the cob and hay, this gave them enough energy to pull the plow for the remaining of the day. We called all the cousins to dinner, sat down at the table and grandfather or grandmother would bless the food. We took about two hours for dinner, after dinner, grandfather would sit on the front porch to smoke his old corn cob pipe, he would read an old current events news paper, the paper was two weeks old at least. Grandmother also smoked a corn cob pipe, they raised their tobacco, they took the wide leaves and stored them in the barn to dry out and to season, he also made his own chewing tobacco by putting layers of leaves and adding molasses between the leaves and let them season. Time was up for dinner brake; grandfather gathered his mules and went back to the field to finish the day. The grey horse was used for special occasions, some time he would allow us to ride the horses, these horses was large animals with huge feet, some of us was afraid to climb on the horses. We sometimes rode the horses to the grocery store. On the way back from the grocery store, we would often meet others sharing the long, narrow gravel road, we would then pull to the shoulders of the road and into the ditch, the road became dusty and visibility was limited, the horses became nervous and jittery we had to come to a complete stop and let the vehicle pass by us. There were two of us per horse and they seem not to have any trouble in carrying double or the saddle bags with merchandise in it. It was one hr. ride there and back. When arriving back to the farm, we would take the merchandise and sit on the front porch, then take the horses back to the barn, unsaddle them and turn them a loose. Every one was glad to see us return safely. This was a beginning of trust being in the young cousins. Grandfather said that we had done well.

Saturday; the day to make ice cream, we all took turns in churning the ice cream, the ice was broken and chipped so the ice would fit all around the mixing cream tube, all the ingredients were in the tube so we churned away, did it until the ingredients were frozen. This was some of the best ice cream that you could ever eat. All enjoyed the ice cream feast. Sunday, we all went to church, the same old church that I had gone to years before moving to Jackson, same old school room that I had once gone to, and the old grave yard in the rear of the church. Food was prepared after church services, we ate and had fun, shortly after dinner, we had to load up the wagon and head back to the farm. When we arrived back to the farm we unloaded the wagon and fed the horses then they were turned loose so they could run and have fun.

Monday; Grandfather was ready for another week in the fields, he would go out to some of the areas that had been planted to see how the crops were doing. I saw grandmother pray for rain for the crops, the rain did come and she thanked God for sending the rain for their crops. The lightning and thunder were very loud and scary, we found shelter under the bed or any place else that would protected us from flying objects. Grandmother said for "all to be quiet" and let God do his work. We all obeyed, soon the storm passed over and we began to come from our hiding places. Too muddy to do any field work, we just hang out around the farm house. The fields began to dry, we took the hoe to the field to chop grass from around the plants, it took at least three days for the fields to completely dry out enough for plowing.

Crops came up and grew; soon it would be harvest time for some of the crops, the garden included. When harvest time came we gathered all of the products that grand- mother would can and store away for the hard winter months. Among these canned products, were peaches, pears, peas, beans, tomatoes, okra, corn and other produce Meat was on the canned food list also, beef and pork was killed, cooked and canned in quart jars, some meat was stored into the smoke house. The smoke house was a special shed that was built specifically, for storing meat, it had a fire pit in the center of the floor of the smoke house to burn certain kind of wood, wood that would be slow burning and gave out smoke instead of heat, this helped the meat to cook and cure slowly, salt was sprinkled over the meat to keep insects off and to preserve the meat. During the bad season when late fall and winter came, they would have food to eat. On the farm it is always about preparation, work during the spring and summer months to prepare for the hard times. Food for the animals had to be stored also, hay and grain had to be gathered and put into the barn. All live stock was brought into the lot or corral for the winter. Cold during the winter months, some times snow and ice came. Harvest time, we also dug peanuts to put away, potatoes were dug and stored in mounds that we had built for the potatoes so they would not freeze during the cold period. We had done well in helping grandfather and grandmother prepare for winter and hard times. Time was coming when we had to prepare to go back to our perspective designations. Our parents were in route to pick their children up, soon we would be back home and in school. Parents would arrive on Saturday, they would leave at different times on Sunday, before anyone left to go home, and we had a good breakfast and prayer. Asking God for a safe trip back to our homes, grandmother and grandfather would give each family food to take home with them, some canned meats and vegetables, peanuts, potatoes, and a water melon. This time father had purchased another car, 1950 Buick road master, it had much more room than the fleet line

Chevy, and it had a large trunk and more room in the back. We loaded up all of our gifts, said good by and began our trip home. This was a hard thing to do, leaving the farm, all the cousins, uncles and aunts, grandparents. I thought that perhaps we could do the same thing next summer. Before we arrived in Jackson, we made a few stops along the way. We sat along beside the highway to eat the lunch that had been prepared before we left the farm. After eating lunch we resumed our trip to Jackson. A short ride by today's standard. About two hours by the old standard of travel, however, we arrived in Jackson safely, and shortly after would be home, another enjoyable summer, and another one to remember forever.

Prepare for school; Register, buying the necessary material for school, each year in school we would meet more challenges. Until then, we would enjoy what was left of summer, we gathered our friends and talked about summer vacation on the farm, or where ever others had gone or done for the summer. We still had a few weeks to hunt and catch cock roaches for the fishermen. Earning extra money was a good thing for us, in going to the movies on Saturdays. Summer was coming to an end; some new students came to our school in all grades, new teachers and some new administrators. Sister had two years to go until she finishes high school. This would be the last year for her boy friend, Arthur Spires. Samuel, youngest brother seem to be doing well in his school. Eli, second oldest brother went to the same school that I went to and he also seem to be doing well. Father still worked at the steel mill and mother was doing part time domestic work. We were a family that had little, but father made sure that we had food on the table and other things that was important to the family. What father could not afford to buy, mother made extra money to afford it. School had begun and we had the seasonal sports that I would take part in. During the school year, we were limited on what to do and how to make money. Studies and some sports took the day. Cousin Fred, father's oldest nephew had been drafted into the Army, cousin Robert, Fred's brother, moved to Oregon. Uncle John had settled in Portland, Oregon after serving time in the pacific theater during Second World War. He had settled there and invited Cousin Robert to come out there to make a new life for him and his wife. Aunt Louise, had also come west to Oregon, they settled in eastern Oregon. She had married a world war two veteran also, cousin Fred, suffered a head injury in the Korean war, he received a head injury on pork chop hill, during an assault on the hill, a grenade was thrown by the enemy and the fragments hit him in the head, he had to have a steel plate put into his head to correct the injury. He married the sister of Robert's wife. Two brothers married two sisters. They all resided in Portland, Oregon in different communities.

Uncle Henry; father's brother, had been in Portland a few years before Fred and Cousin Robert, he worked at the ship yards and was married to Lucille Johnson, she was also from Mississippi. For Blacks, the Kaiser Ship yards seem to be the place to work. Steel foundries, steel mills were other places Blacks could get good paying jobs. We had relatives leaving Mississippi, seeking better pay and a better way of life for their families, some settled in California, Washington, Illinois, Oregon, and other states. In Jackson, we were doing the same things that had been going on for a long time, working hard and receiving little money. Uncle John had been trying to get father to leave Mississippi, and to come west and start a new life for his family. One day, we had a cousin to come from a town in Mississippi called Flora he came to Jackson to visit us and to spend a day with us. Three off us decided to go to the movies on a school day, we wanted to show our cousin a good time while he was in town, we walked to the movies in the down town area. The police saw us walking to the movies and thought that we should have been in school and they stopped us on the side walk in down town Jackson. We were going to the Alamo theater, the police asked what were we doing out of school, we told them that our cousin was here from Flora to visit us and we were going to the movies to show a good time. Police did not listen, they put all three of us in the back seat of the police car and took us back to school, and they wanted all the students and teachers to see us being brought back to school in a police car. They said bad things to us on the way back to school, Brother Eli, and cousin began to ask questions about being picked up. One police officer shouted to shut up, he said he had not whipped a little nigger's ass in a long time. We knew that he was a racist, we didn't say any thing else. The other police officer told the one that said those racist words that he should not have said to us what he did. Conversation ended and we were back at school. Everyone saw us getting out of the police car thought we had done something wrong; we had to explain what we had made happened. This was the first time that I had any encounter with the police. I began to see just how vicious those people could be. This was an indication of all the things that I had heard off, blacks being harassed and found dead some place; there would be nothing that they would not do. Many blacks had been found dead and deaths not solved. Murderer or murderers were never brought to justice.

Last trip to the farm; not knowing what was in the future, this was the last time we would visit the farm and spend time with grandfather and grandmother. We would not see many of the cousins again. We came together on the farm and as usual, we enjoyed each other, we all had gotten older and grew in size. This was an asset to helping grandfather with some of the chores. Our experience from previous years on the farm gave us more knowledge in what needed to be done, we were all eager to help. Working during the week when the weather was good, plowing the fields, planting the crops. When harvest time came, we helped grandfather and grandmother. This would be the last summer we would spend on the farm and to spend time with our grandparents. All work on the farm was completed, and we began to gather hay and grain for the animals and store them in the barn. Grandmother would start her yearly canning of food that would sustain them through out the winter months. When chores were done, we went to the big pond to fish for cat fish and perch. We went over the hill to visit our great aunt and great uncle. This is where our cousin lived. "Sugar man", was called this name because he loved to eat sugar cane, he stayed energetic all the time from eating much sugar cane. We played games and had fun. This would be the last time that I would see him for a long time. Parents were coming soon to pick their children up and take them home, this was the worst time off all having to leave grand- father, grandmother, cousins, and the farm animals.

Parents arrived on Saturday; we all came together to celebrate this special occasion. We made ice cream and ate lunch before we departed, each family left at different times, some lived far, and some lived near. My family left early, because we had to travel back to Jackson. The old Buick road master was loaded and ready to roll, things that had been given to us by our grandparents to take back with us. There were a few stops made before we arrived back home, we stopped along the highway to stretch and eat snacks, thirty minutes was taken out of the trip. After relaxing and finishing up our snacks, we resumed the trip; the next stop would be home. After arriving home, the first thing that we done were to unload all the merchandise and put them away. Finishing these chores, we asked if we could go and play, finding our friends and getting together. We walked, and talked about our summer vacation. We also talked about the new school year, what we expected out of the year and what sports we wanted to play, classes that we liked most and our favorite teachers. With three weeks to go before school started, we tried to get as much fun in as we could. Playing cow boys and Indians running through tall grass, I stepped on a broken beer bottle and nearly cut the left heel off on the left foot, I could not walk on the foot and friends had to piggy back me back home. Mother and Aunt Rosetta, rushed me to the Doctor. He stopped the bleeding and examined the foot, checking for any broken glass that might be lodged in the heel. There were none, so the Doctor cleaned and stitched the heel up. Mother and Aunt Rosetta brought me back home. This was a big blow, I could not finish the summer the way that I had wished to do. Healing had to take place; I had to stay off the foot much as possible. Friends came to the house to visit me. When school started, I was able to register and start classes on time. This summer had been a combination of good and bad. Having a good time on the farm and coming home and suffering an injury. However, the injury did not stop me from attending my classes; it did stop me from playing sports for that season. I could not run or make quick moves on the foot, when games were played and my school was playing, I had to sit on the side line to help cheer them on to a win. I was able to go to the movies with my sister and her boy friend, Arthur Spires. My brother, Eli and my self, still had to go along with sister and her date to the movies. We knew where to sit and the usual things to do. As long as we could buy popcorn and hot dogs, we were contented, when the movies were over and we walked home, we went inside and left sister and her friend to themselves, they usually, sat on the front porch until it was time to come in the house. Mother would not go to sleep until we all were inside of the house. Friend left and return to his home across the railroad tracks in west Jackson. He had a job that he had to go to on Monday morning. Her friend had graduated two years earlier, and this would be the last year for sister attending high school, plans had already been made between sister and her boy friend. It is time to face all facts; we are growing up and fast becoming young adults. School was coming along very well for all of us, sister's last year in school and was looking forward to graduation. My foot was healing fast and soon I would be back to normal.

Relatives leaving Mississippi; many relatives were leaving the state, going elsewhere to seek a better life for their families. To work and receive a good salary, only leaving the south would offer this opportunity. A Black Korean war veteran had come back from Korea, when he got back from fighting the war, something had gone wrong with him and some white folks, and he became angry and killed a white man. The hunt was on to catch him, he escaped through the woods, and they used hounds to try to track him. Finally, the dogs caught scent of where he was, each time a dog or sheriff's deputy would come in so far into the woods, he would shoot them in the fore head, many law officers and hounds lost their lives in trying to capture him. They never did capture him, they said that they set the" woods on fire" to flush him out, but they never found his body. This soldier had fought the enemy in Korea, only to come home and find the real enemy was here, your country men. No one knew what happened to Eddie Noel, he could have escaped to another State. Many things happened throughout the south, people came up missing and never found. Uncle John had been trying to get father to come out west where he was to start a new life for him and his family. It would take three years before father took serious what uncle John was telling him to do.

25

Sister Graduated; she received her high school diploma from Lanier High School, west Jackson. This was a happy occasion for all of us, the first to graduate from high school. Mother finished the eight grades, and father only finished the third grade. This truly, was a joyous occasion. She would live in Jackson for one more year. I was thinking of other things to do, other places to go and see some other part of the country, two years later, father told us what his plans were for the future, he would take Uncle John's" advice to leave Mississippi" He told father to let him know two weeks in advance before he come so he would have a job waiting for him when he arrived. Sister was asked by her friend to marry him. He left Jackson and went to Flint, Michigan to work for general motors. One year later, sister left for Michigan to marry her long time boy friend. She arrived there and a week later, they became husband and wife. My parents kept in contact with them until the marriage and they were settled in. There were other things taking place in Jackson, accidents were happening and people were dying. There were unsolved murders, there were hate by all.

Whites and blacks were killing one another. One thing that motivated father to leave was the murder of a young black boy from Chicago, who had come down to visit his grandparents in a small town in Mississippi. The lie that was told by a white woman was that he had whistled at her from the opposite side of the street, she went home and told her husband that lie; this was enough to bring his buddies together and plot on what to do about it. They came to his grandparent's home and took him away. His where about was not known until a few weeks later. These people had murdered the young boy and threw his body into the Pearl River, they found concrete tied to his feet so he would never come to the surface, Government divers found his body. The husband or his friends were never convicted of the crime. Our parents wanted us to stay near where we live, didn't want us to be accused of something that was negative. There could be white people riding around the neighborhood looking for trouble, we kept a three block radius from where we lived. We still played our usual games, playing marbles, throwing coins. When we wanted to do something different, we would go to the cookie house which was on the corner of

Mill and sideway street, you could buy a bag of cookies for five cents, there would be cookies of all kind that you could purchase peanut butter, coca nut, oat meal/raisin and other kinds. The bakery sold those cookies that they would not send to grocery stores and other places, so they had imperfections, broken and other imperfections. To us they looked like cookies, smelled like cookies and could not tell what the difference was. Cookies were only broken and did not come out as a whole cookie so these were sold at a fraction of what whole cookies would cost.

Sitting on the long concrete steps of the cookie house, we ate cookies and counted cars that would pass by on mill, during this time, there were not many other makes of cars, trucks on the road. Ford, general motors, American motor, and one or two more manufacturers. When a vehicle would approach from a distance, just within hearing distance, we would ask one another what is the make of that vehicle. We were able to tell whether it was a ford, Chevy, dodge, we could even tell whether it was a v-8, or 6 cylinder ,the sound of the engine was all we had to hear to determine the make of the vehicle, However, we could not tell the year of the vehicle. All makes of vehicles had their own distinctive sound. Families in the community were cautious in allowing their children to stray too far out of the area in which they lived. There were obvious reasons why. Three weeks went by after the crimes had been committed and the parents allowed us to venture a little farther out. We were allowed to catch cock roaches and mow lawns for extra money. Pass word for going around neighbors homes to catch roaches, was to say" roach boy" loud and clear, to let them know that we were not burglars or some one else that were not wanted. We washed cars on sunny days. Enough money was made to go to the movies and to buy popcorn, ice cream, and to eat hot dogs. These were the usual ways of making extra money, sometime our parents would give us two or three dollars as a good will gift, if they had it to give to us. Any money given to us was appreciated.

Father had received a letter from his brother in Gary, Indiana. Uncle Pearl, asked him to come up there and live, he said he could get him a job at the" steel mill where he worked", father accepted and went north to Gary, Indiana, to live and work with uncle Pearl. He started work on Monday, two days after his arrival and worked there for six months, before the plant started to lay employees off. Father would send money home to mother to take care of the expensive around the house. The seventh month, father returned home and went back to his old job at contractor's material steel mill. Few months at home, he received a long distance phone call from his brother out west. Uncle John, who had been trying to get father to come out west for some time, finally, accepted to come out there. He told Uncle John when he would leave Jackson, as requested by Uncle John. He wanted to have a job ready for him, when he arrived. Uncle John had apartments that he owned, soon there would be a vacancy, and father and family would have some place to live. School had started and many things had to be in order. Father left Jackson, about one month after Uncle John had called him to confirm his coming. We did not want to see father leave us again, but we knew he was leaving to make a better life for his family. He left behind a wife and three sons. The day father arrived in Portland, Oregon, a phone call came and told mother that he had" arrived safely", after three days and two nights aboard the Great Northern rail train. He had seen some off the most beautiful country in the world. His trip was an enjoyable one. Date was set for the rest of the family to join him, sister and her husband were also notified of when we would be leaving Jackson, and heading to Oregon. My long journey started when I left Mississippi. Before we left, we had to come together with our friends and relatives that would be left behind. This was one of the hardest times of my life, leaving relatives and friends behind and going to the other side of the United States they did not want to see us leave either. If a better life was in the making for us, then father had to do what ever it took to get us there. One thing for sure, Jackson, Mississippi was not the answer. Mother had gotten things in order and we were ready to take the long journey, tickets had been purchased, a basket full of food had been prepared, housing contents were sold and some given away. Uncle Sonny, father's oldest brother took us to the train station. There we waited to board the City of New Orleans train to

Chicago, Illinois, where after a four hour wait we would board the Great Northern rail west bound. While waiting, mother's twin sister, Aunt Oral came to the train station to say by. There would be many years before we see her again, many pleasant memories of her and her family coming to the farm at grandparent's farm. Her children and her twin sister's children had many memories to cherish. Soon the train would be coming and we had to say by. A prayer was asked for a safe trip then she and her daughter departed.

Train arrived and we began to board, we sat up high in the dome, good visibility all around, both, sides of train. This would be a very long trip, there would be much to see and we wanted to see as much as we could. Country folks, we had never left Mississippi, this was a whole new world to me. We came through snow in most of the States that we traveled through, Minnesota, North Dakota, Montana, Idaho, Washington and Oregon, troublesome part of the trip, coming through Montana, deep snow and high mountains. We encountered trouble with some of the steep terrain and deep snow. The engine stalled, going up a steep incline, the train had to wait in place for three or four hours until another engine arrived with a snow plow out front to push the snow off the tracks. After the engine hook up, the train continued the trip, traveling at a very low speed. Slowly, we crept up the mountain and down the other side, very slow coming down the mountain, there were ice and snow everywhere. It took all day and all that night to come through Montana. It was beautiful scenery; we saw mountain goats, mountain sheep, elk, and many deer. We arrived in Sand Point, Idaho early the next morning, it did not take very long to come across this small section of the State, and it also had some beautiful scenery, entering into Washington State. There were yet more beautiful scenery, jagged mountains, Cascade Mountains, and the long, wide river of the Columbia, we were told of the history of the river and some of the great people that traveled the river, Great people such as Lewis and Clark, The river starts in Canada as a small trickle of a river and get wider, deeper as the river runs into the Pacific Ocean, the mighty Pacific Ocean. We traveled nearly, all day coming through Washington State.

Arrived in Vancouver, WA was the last stop before entering Portland, Oregon, the train came across the mighty Columbia and into the Central Rail station. Father, and his brother, Uncle John were there to meet us. The big, nine passenger station wagon was loaded and we headed to our new resident. The apartment house was one of a few houses that Uncle John had purchased. Portland had been good to him. He and his wife, Aunt Della Mae, had done well in Portland; she had a good paying job working at the ship yard. We arrived at the apartment where we would be living. This was on the same street that Uncle John and his wife lived, only a few houses from where we would be living only a few houses from the popular, union avenue. This is one of the busy streets that Blacks usually travel on. The apartment that we had was a huge apartment; it had enough room for all of us to be comfortable. Cousin Fred and cousin Robert lived across union avenue on the same street that we and uncle John lived on, they also rented a house from uncle John, they all worked at a steel mill or foundry. Uncle Henry, another one of father's brothers, he and his family lived on Mississippi. Another popular street for blacks to go and do business, Aunt Lu La, father's sister, she and her family lived on grand avenue, about two miles from where we were living. They all left Mississippi before we did, and they had been established with a home and a job. Many members of the Bryant's family had left the south; they had re- located in other places, such as California, Washington, Oregon and some other States. We still had many relatives on father's side of the family to remain in Mississippi until this day. Maybe they did not have confident of moving to a foreign land, or all of the memories that they had of their child hood, but what ever the reason for not leaving, they choose to remain there. We had arrived in Portland at the end of April, it was drizzling rain and it was cool, snow was melting and spring was coming. The City of Portland looked just as beautiful as Uncle John had described. Only one month to go before school would be out for the summer, so I waited for the fall to enroll in classes. There were choices of which school I wanted to attend. Benson Polytechnic, a school for boys, Grant High school, Washington and Jefferson High schools. After much thought and consideration, I decided to attend the all boys' school. I registered in the freshmen class at the age of fourteen. This was a highly technical school and any one could not attend there, you had to have a higher score to attend and to keep a high score to remain there. Students from all over the tri-county area could attend. It had very good athletes and offered many sports. School had good representation in all sports. I did not take part in any of the organized sports.

The hard transition from a segregated all Black school to a racially intermixed school was something that I had to work hard on to over come and to feel comfortable in that environment, few black students and no black teachers. There were only 100 Blacks in the whole school of 3,000 students. This was mentally a long journey, the adjustment of mixed classmates. Everyone treated me well, it was not a big deal to them, they had been around blacks, most understood blacks and where they came from. I had no problem with any of the white students. The biggest challenge was to myself, I didn't know how I would be received by the other students, fitting in was a personal battle. Half way through the school year, I began to feel more confident and more comfortable in my surroundings. As time went on, I began to make friends, one of my closest friends was Jack J. Johnson, he lived nearly a mile from where I lived. We became the very best of friends, we walked to school together along with his first cousin, Billy Bridges, and we had fun in getting to know each other better. When school was out for the summer, we made extra money by going to the bean fields and the berry fields; we earned money in lawn mowing and other chores. I had begun to learn more about the city in which I live and started to like it. Jack took me to his house and introduced me to his parents, sisters and an older brother, they were very nice people and they made me feel welcome. During the same day, I took him to be introduced to my parents, he was very manly and respectable, and my parents approved of him. He was introduced to my uncle and aunt and my cousins. I told him about the one sister that I had in Flint, Michigan, and that she had recently gotten married. Mother and sister stayed in contact with one another and she wanted to come out to Portland in the near future.

Chapter Three

We walked up and down the avenues, William and Vancouver. These were the main streets that Blacks were patronizing; these streets had good restaurants, ice cream parlors, bakeries, dry goods, grocery, theaters, shoe repair shops, and much more. We had to leave the community to work and to go to school but other than that, we were much sustained. Down town Portland, was a beautiful, clean area, it had much more to offer and to see. Having many choices of what theater, and which movies we wanted to see. There was one of three theaters in the black community called the Egyptian Theater it was located on Union, the theater was only a few blocks from where I lived. Jack would show me around to different places and to meet other people, some of them became good friends. Mother and father had been learning the city also, they would ride through some of the most beautiful areas surrounding where we lived. God had already shown mother the house that she would own, he told her that" this house would be for her and her family to own and to live in", she was a strong Christian person that believed in every thing that God reveals to her. 'She said that" God had shown her this particular house that would become her family's home. She described the house as being very large in size, white in color, and was sitting on a hill; it had four bed rooms, bath room up stairs, hall way, wide stair well with winding rails. Down stairs there was a long front porch half roofed and the other half was for sun enjoyment, The short hall way before you entered the large living room, it also had a large dining room and a good sized kitchen, there was a full sized basement to the house, all of this God had shown her, and he told her this would be the house for her family". Less than one year, mother claimed the house that was in her dream that God had shown her. Before we were ready to move, sister had called mother and said her' husband had been laid off his job at the auto manufactory", mother wanted nothing more than to be with her daughter again. She told her about the house that god had revealed to her and for her to come on out west, there would be a place for her family and father and uncle would try to obtain a job for her husband. When they arrived some three or four weeks later, we were still living in Uncle John's apartment house. We all lived together, there were another member in the family, and sister had her first child, a healthy baby boy, less than three months old. He was a beautiful child. Father had spoken to his foreman and supervisor concerning a job for his son in law. One week had passed and sister's husband was called to come to work at the same company and in the department that father worked in, this was a good thing that they would work together in the same department. These Blessings came from God.

Moving; this was the "dream house that was shown to mother in her dream, it was identical to the one that was in her dream". We all moved into the big house. Mother gave thanks to God for showing her the house that would be for her and family's home. We settled in and began to enjoy our surroundings, this was on n.e.10th. Ave., our family was one of the first black families to live on this street or any where east of 7th are. When school started, I continued to go to Benson high school, closer yet to school, Jack my friend, would continue to come by so we could walk to school together. This year, walking would not be as easy for us as it had been in past year; we had to bypass a major construction project. They were building one of the largest shopping centers in America. We had to walk 4 or 5 blocks out of the way to get to school, this would be one of the largest in the world, and people from around the globe would come to Portland to see the mall when completed. The same route was used to go to school and to come home after school. We were young men and soon we would be interested in girls, we were now in our second year of high school and there were no girls at the school that we were going to. We went to basketball and foot ball games in order to meet some nice young girls. Dating white girls was a no, and to think of dating any girl, white or black at this stage of the game. First you had to find the girl that was interested in you, and you had to be approved by the parents and other siblings. Young ladies were well respected, and if not, her brother or cousins would have a talk with you. In the near future, parents would ease the restrictions on some of the older girls.

Having house parties; Parents would sometimes allow their daughters and sons to go to a specific house where there were adults that would over see the party so it would not get out of hand. The boy, who was to pick the young lady up, was to come into the house and greet the parents, tell them when you are expected to have her back home and where the party would be located, the agreement had to be obeyed. You wanted to do the right thing toward the parents so when asked for her to go to another party, they would hardly 22object. The parties that we had were respectable and orderly. If and when a disruptive person or persons would arrive at the party, they were immediately, ask to leave the premises. They usually left without any confrontation. Most parties were held in the basement of the house, the basement was decorated as to look like a club house or entertainment center, the host would put much effort in making the guests comfortable, sometime there would be more than one party at different locations in the community, they would be on the same night. People sometime went from one to the other to see where all the action was. Regardless of which party you would choose, they all had fun and gave them something to talk about the next day. Periodically, we would have these parties going on the entire year. Eli, had his own friends that he hung out with, during their own thing, he made friends with boys around his age that lived on or near where we lived. He loved dogs, dogs of any breed. One day Eli had gotten a huge German Shepard dog that would not allow father to come into the house after he had come home from work. The dog would bark and show his disapproval of him coming near the door of the house. Eli, had to come to father's rescue, otherwise, the dog would not let father in the house. We never knew where Eli had found the dog. Father was tired after working all day in a hot, dusty steel foundry and he became angry at Eli and the dog. He told Eli," never bring another stray dog to the house". Eli never did bring another dog to the house. However, he continued to love dogs and made friends with many of them. Samuel, the baby of the family, was too young to be given too much liberty; he had to stay on the same block that we lived on to play with the friends that he had made. His friends to this day; are Frank Jones, Richard Folks and a few more. Eli friends were; Thomas Hartley, the Austin boys, and a few more. These mentioned were their closet friends, school that Eli and Samuel attended and it was only a few blocks away from where we lived. We all had made friends with people around our same age and attended the same school together. My nephew, Marvin Spires was growing, he was our first, grand child, nephew or niece born to our family, we all loved him and treated him with care and attention, Mother and father was especially proud of their first grand child, and he was a boy, something that they had hoped for. On Sunday we would attend the Vancouver Baptist Church, the very first church that we attended since moving to Portland, Oregon. After attending Vancouver Baptist for one year, we left and attended the Method Church of God and Christ. We still attend this church until this day, the location and name has been changed, but the members and the traditions mostly, remain.

Last year at Benson Polytechnic School, my friend and I decided that this would be the last year that we would attend the all boys' school, we wanted to have females' companions, and the technical school did not offer this opportunity to do so. Our choice were to attend Grant High School, the distance would be a little farther from where we live but you didn't care, the scenery was prettier and we could talk to both, boys and girls. The school year at Benson was much the same as the year before, much class work and many sports to participate in if you choose to do so. I chose not to play any organized sports at school but decided to try out for the community center's basketball team, there were less competition there than in school organized sports. The community center offered boxing, wrestling, basketball, softball, volley ball and more. They also had some special events periodically, dance, and parties. Knot street community was the name of this community center; it was in the heart of the Black community. There were more community centers that were frequently patronized by Black youths. There were a few parks in the general area that we could go and play baseball or foot ball. Irving Park was the closet to where we lived and it was the most frequented, if you felt energetic and did not mind walking; you could walk to the Peninsula Park. When school was out or on the week end, we would take the long walk to go to other parks. We could not spend much time during school days at any park; we had to be home to finish our school work and to prepare for the next day. Shopping mall is half finished; this would be the place of interest.

School is out for the season; Finding a way to earn money for the summer months. On a beautiful, sunny day we would go to the car wash to see if we would be hired to wash or dry cars off. Some times he or she would tell us to hang around and it would be a chance for us to work for a few hours, it all depended how busy they became. The most popular car wash for us was the Holly wood hub and car wash co. This was the closet to where we live, car wash was on Broadway and Williams, all of the businesses would close at that time. There would be a few drug stores that would remain open for emergencies. A few gas stations remained open also. If you did not do what you needed to do by six p.m. Saturday evening, you would have to wait until Monday morning. Fridays night and Saturday nights were the" go to the strip time", most people would congregate on these predominantly, Black streets, they would drive up and down each one of these streets to see or to be seen by some one that they knew. Many restaurants, clubs and other entertainment establishments, there was a park between William and Vancouver this is where many would congregate. Sidewalks fill with people traveling up and down the avenue. Some would take a trip across the Willamette river into the down town area, they would ride the streets of down town Portland. Portland had many bridges, all extending across the Willamette River into the west part of Portland. Industrial complexes dominated most of the west side of Portland. When harvest time was ready, we would go to pick strawberries, beans. We also had fun fishing in the many Rivers and lakes that were surrounding the County area. This was a clean, beautiful City. As time went by, we began to explore more of the State. Uncle John and father would take us fishing, there was an Island that was in the northern part of the county that nestled between two bodies of water, the Columbia and the Willamette Rivers, this place was a good place to fish and to purchase farm produce, all farm land. It was rich in the history of Oregon, there had been many battles fought with Native Americans and the people that settled in this part of the State. The Island was taken and settlers claimed the land, history abounds Oregon. Uncle John and Uncle Henry took us many places through out the State, we traveled to the Pacific coast, this was as far as we could go and still be on land in the United States. To me, this was like looking at another world, the huge blue ocean, the high tides and ocean waves were a beautiful thing to see. We followed the Columbia all the way to the ocean; this is where the Columbia runs into the mighty Pacific Ocean. Astoria, Oregon, this is where the river meet the Ocean.

Summer vacation came to an end, and we were preparing for school, buying a different style of clothing and coming to school in the latest clothing, Khakis and Blue jeans with starch and being creased. I am not sure what all of this had with you learning, but this was the fad at that time. However, we were in high school and older, we had to be properly dressed and carried ourselves as responsible teens. We now would be in the presence of young ladies and we wanted to give a good impression to them. We walked home from school, girls and boys together, talking of different things along the way. We talked of what we had done for the summer, when and where the next party would be given. A few students were allowed to drive their parent's car to school on special days, many students, jammed into the huge car, students sitting on students. Gladly, the parents of the driver didn't see all of us jammed into their car like we were. I knew I had to study for my drivers permit, I wanted a car, we had to impress the young ladies and show them that we could drive a car and our chances of finding a young lady would increase. The White students had cars, some owned their cars, and some used their parent's car. Some even drove old pick up trucks. Chevrolet, Ford and some time a Dodge truck would show up on school campus. Most students worked on their own vehicles, super tuning them so they would take off fast and burn tires in doing so, they wanted to impress the other students. I knew the only way that I could get a car; I would have to work hard, save my money and purchase one. First, I had to pass my Drivers examination. I studied hard and passed the juvenile exam, now I was ready to learn how to drive and to handle a car.

Father used to take me some place where there were no traffic, he taught me all the instruments and what they were for, he taught me how to turn, brake, park, and to change gears. I had a few lessons before he let me have the wheel by my self. I had a good teacher, father would not turn me loose until he was absolutely sure that I could handle the car, even then he would be sitting beside me. Father had a 54 Pontiac Catalina, this was a good car, and I learned to drive it, some time my Brother in Law would take me out for further training. We went out to Portland Meadows, where they had a large parking lot, built for horse racing and dog racing fans. We used the parking area when there were no races on that day. I found work after school for a few hours a day and a few days per week, I earned enough money in that time to purchase my first car, this was a 1949, ford coupe two door hard top, 6, cylinder with a standard three speed transmission. The car ran good for about two months, and then I began to have problems with it. Cold weather came and it contributed to the crack in the block, the engine would not hold water, the car remained parked in front of our house until father and I could figure out what to do with it. I was still working, earning money and saving what I could. The car remained parked for nearly a year before we knew what we would do with it. I had worked most of the summer and school was fast approaching, I wanted to purchase another car or get that one fixed that I had. Father insisted to wait for the next summer, that way I would have enough money to purchase a better car. The school year rolled by and summer was nearly, upon us. I had done well in school and still worked part time in the evenings, Father and I begun to visit car dealer ships, trying to find something that would fit my budget and dependable. After visiting many car lots, we found a beautiful 1955 Chevrolet Bell air, 2dr, hard top, two tone color, red and white. This car was equipped with an automatic transmission; this car looked good and had a good engine. We all liked the way it looked. The old ford was traded off, and we purchased the Bell Air, I drove the car home, father then took it for a short drive, he liked the way the car drove and we were satisfied. I passed my drivers test for a regular drivers license, now I could drive to work and else where. I worked for the Bradley Pie Company for the remainder of the summer, I then left, finished my last year in school, graduated and started work at the same steel foundry that my father, uncle, and brother in law were employed. I started to get serious, I wanted to find a decent young lady, someone that I could be true to and she is true to me, I did not like to be going from one girl to the next. They say that "nothing good comes easy." I met my would be wife after a long wait and prayer, I asked God to help me to find someone that would be true to me, and I be true to her, God had me in his plans.

I met a young lady at a friend's house party, the host of the party, was the school mate and neighbor of the young lady that I was to meet at the party, they went to school together, in the same classes, she still was in school at Washington High school. This was a perfect opportunity to meet her, my friend's first cousin's friend, and neighbor. I went to the party; I met the young lady and fell in love with her at first eye contact. I did not know what to say to her, I was introduced to her and we greeted each other, after that, I looked for something to say, making sure I did not say anything that would offend her. She was the most beautiful girl that I had ever seen, perhaps it was puppy love or maybe it really was the work of God's answer to my prayer. Dating her did not come easy, for many times that I had called to speak with her, she would tell her brothers or her sisters to tell me that she would not be home. I did not give up and not become discouraged, my sights were set high and I had honed in on her, she might have tried to run away from me, but she could not hide, I was persistent, and continued my chase after her. Through talking with her older sister Mar, she convinced her to talk to me on the phone when ever I called for her. Talking to her sister must to have done some good; the next time that I called I was able to make a date with her. I went to her house on n. Page and n. Flint in front of the grade school that they had attended. I kept the 1955 Chevy clean and ready for the potential date.

I arrived at her resident, got out knocked on the door and introduced my self to one of her brothers, he said to wait for a minute until he returned, I was asked to come in and meet the parents. They all seemed to approve of me. The first date, Mar her older sister, was the one that had helped me to get a date with her, Mar asked if it would be OK if she could come along with us on this first date?. I said sure" I would not think of saying anything else, I did not want to blow this chance." We rode around and explored the city, and we went out to the suburbs to purchase hamburgers and eat ice cream. This first date was a good date. I believe, Mar wanted to come along with us to see what kind of person that I was. She did give her stamp of approval and this was the start of something good. From this point on I didn't have any more problems in her dating me.

Introducing my date to my family; when my family saw what I had been chasing all of this time, they were astonished and happy to meet a beautiful young lady such as her and she told mother and father her name and "her family's origination". Sister and her husband seem to approve of her to. Soon sister and their family would be moving into their new house that they had built and they would be living in a rural area of north Portland, known as the Saint Johns area, Arthur, her husband had been working for a year and they saved their money to have their dream house built. Eli, the second oldest son was suffering with his diabetics and mother had to prepare special diets for him to eat, she had to test his sugar level at least four times a day, his activities were limited, and his schooling was limited also. After a long bout with the disease, his kidneys began to weaken, he lived with this disease for twelve years, he eventually, had to be hospitalized, and water had to be drained from the kidneys. This was a brave young boy; he loved everyone, including animals. It was very hard to see a young man so energetic and so caring and loving would be afflicted with such Illness. Mother stayed on her knees praying to God for his healing, he began to worsen and he had to visit the hospital more frequently, and he passed away at home at the age of 21, this was a terrible blow to the family and to his friends. So young, so loving and caring for everyone seem if though it wasn't for real. The brother I loved so dearly had left us, all the things we had done in Mississippi, on grandfather's farm. In Jackson when he threw two tar cans into the fire and they exploded, burning the three of us in the process. Eli, our beloved brother would no longer be with us. We all took his passing very hard, Mother especially, took it hard. As time went by, we knew he would not come back, so we overcame the best way we could. Mother had consistency praying for him and she never gave up hope. She believed that God had a plan to take him out of this world and into a more peaceful place. She believed that he went to Heaven to be God and other relatives.

My girlfriend came over to the house to sit and talk with mother, trying to ease her mind about her son. Mae is my girl friend's name, she like talking to Eli before he took sick and passed away. I was still working at the Electric Steel Foundry, and had joined the Oregon Army National Guard for a six month tour of training at Fort Ord, California, this time away gave me time to get my mind off what had happen in the family. It gave me a chance to meet other people from across the Nation. We trained with the Regular Army Troops for that six month period. The training was very hard, much running, marching, firing rifles and machine guns, throwing hand grenades, taking gas and chemical courses. We had to march for twenty four hours. When we arrived at our destination, we had to pitch a two man pulp tent and we had to choose another soldier to pitch the tent with, it was night and the only light that we had was the moon light, we pitched the tents and dug a trench around the tent to keep rain or moisture from making a mud puddle at the entrance of the tent. Three or four, we had to rise and shine, we had to do pt., and run five miles before we would be called to chow. One night we got back from a field exercise and went to our tent to rest up, there was a rattle snake in the tenth, the area around our tent were evacuated and we began to flush the snake out of the tent, with m-80 fire crackers, the snake came out angry, he was trying to jump on anyone that was in his way of escape. We finally killed the snake with blank rifle cartridges and m-80 fire crackers. When our camping out and going through the field exercises was over, we strike tents and loaded the supplies on deuce and a half trucks and, we marched back to our barracks. It was called the 48 hour death march. We had been running, walking, run; walk all the way back to the main garrison.

Company Commander; it was good to see that our commander was a Black officer, 1st, lieutenant from O. C. S., he loved to run, my platoon sergeant was also Black. The U.S. Army had not been long racially mixed, during the Korean War when it became fully interracially mixed. There were still many racist individuals in the Army. Many came from all over the country and brought their racial views and attitudes with them. Some from the south and never been in a racially mixed surroundings. Their true feeling would come out when ever they would go to the base PX. And loaded up on beer, they would come back to the barracks and started talking racial. It took alcohol to boost their true feeling; many had never been around any other race of people except their own race. People of many races were in the U.S. Army, all depended upon each other to carry out their missions and their survival. I suppose I was lucky in one respect, I came into the Army at a time, there were no war, I was in between wars. After the Korean war and before the Vietnam war. When the Vietnam War started my enlistment was up. I served 12 years with the Oregon National Guard and left as a buck sergeant. During my stay at Fort Ord, I saw much history. On week ends, we sometimes went to San Francisco and visited China town, San Jose, Salinas, Monterey and Mexico. I saw much, and I learned much, mostly about people and how they lived, and some of their thoughts. After four months of training, we earned a two week vacation, we all left and went our own way, some went home to spend time, and some stayed in California. I came home to be with my family and to see my new girl friend. I caught the Trail Ways bus to come back to Portland. When I arrived I had a bad cold and mother insisted that I go to the doctor and check the cold out. Dr. Marshal diagnosed me of having a "touch of pneumonia". I was glad mother persuaded me to go to the Doctor. The Doctor gave me medication I began to feel better; he also wrote a letter to my commanding officer, informing him of my condition. During my stay at home, I was able to spend time with my girl friend.

43

In my shopping in China town, I purchased gifts for mother and my girl friend, they were glad to receive the gifts. When time came for me to return back to active duty, mother and girl friend took me back to the bus station, we all said" good by, and they would be praying for me". I finished the two months that I had left and graduated with the rest of the Company. We hated to leave friends, but we all wanted out and go home to our love ones. I begun my long trip home, this time for good, I would only have to go to drills two week ends per month and a two weeks of summer training each year.

When I arrived, all were glad to see me and to know I had completed my mission in the Army. I would take a week off before I returned back to work. I wanted to un-wind and enjoy family and girl friend before going back to work. My friend and I continued to have fun, playing ball at the community center and going to house parties. My 1955 Chevy was running good, and we used to drive up and down the Avenues to see what was happening. At that time, any one who had a car had a name printed on the side of it. People knew who you were when they saw a particular name on the side of your car. There were many titles of songs, name of movies, and stars. My ride name was" Handy Man" named after a title of a song, when people saw me coming they would yell out "Handy Man "and they needed a ride or to sit and talk. When they called out, most of the time we would stop and pick them up. Many times, we just went to a tavern and played pool or fool's ball, we some times had a beer or two. I never got used to drinking beer, I never liked the smell or the taste of it, and we sat and talked, enjoying each other's company. My friend and I doubled dated; he had met a young lady that lived on the same street that I live, three blocks from my parents. I had seen her before, and she had attended the same high school that we had gone to. We would go to her home to talk with her mother, a sister and her brother; we played old records and watched television. There weren't very many Blacks in Portland, and we knew most of them. However, there were a very few of them living elsewhere, other towns in other counties, but 98 percent lived in Portland.

Back to work; all of my fellow workers were glad to see me return, they wanted me to tell them of my military training and some of the things I had done. I told them that it was the" best experience that I could have received. Army truly made a difference in my life; it gave me a feeling of independence". I believed that I was ready for the responsibilities of becoming a man. I worked at my old job that I had before I went into the service, worked there for three months before I was promoted to the upper core room. Started out servicing core makers, keeping them supplied with sand and steel plates for the cores. When the cores were loaded onto a huge steel rack and then put into a huge oven to be cooked. It was a good experience, working my way to becoming a core maker. I would become the first Black core maker that ever worked in the upper core room. All of the fellow workers respected me and I respected them. My foreman and my lead man they both, liked me and was giving me more responsibilities. The dept. had received a new shell core machine that would make and cook cores on the same machine, it took a completely different type of sand to blow in to the core boxes, the core boxes were aluminum alloy and would cook the core in the box, the cores would not have to be put into the ovens, saving time and labor. The machines were eventually, accepted and put on the core production line. The company was a good place to work during that time, the pay was good, the benefits were fair and many people wanted to work there. During Christmas, the company gave a party; you could bring your family and friends to the party. Once a year, they had a stag party with only men allowed to attend. The company's picnic, male or female, family and friends were all invited. Making more money than I had ever earned before, I saved and helped father and mother with their expensive. Girl friend and I could go to a better restaurant and attend a better theater. Soon I would trade my old 1955, Chevy off and purchase a New 1959 Chevy, Impala, this was a beautiful, black with all around chrome, white wall tires, maroon up-holster. It had a 308, V-8, Engine. Even chose a name for it,"Mr. Personality", was the name that was chosen. Everyone seem to like the Impala, when they saw me coming, they would yell out, "hey Mr. Personality" wait for me, I would most of the time stop and talk to them or give them a ride to their destination. Girl friend became jealous and did not want me to pick up other people, especially, other females, even though they were some one I knew. I knew she cared for me more than she let on to; she also liked the new impala also. However, the practice did quit and I was very selective in who I let ride.

Relatives passing on; this seems to be a domino's effect, every two years there would be a relative passing on. Father's oldest brother in Mississippi had passed, two years later his oldest sister passed away, and two or three years had gone by, father's youngest brother passed. Uncle John, he was the one who was responsible for us to be in Portland, Oregon, he is the one that helped father get a job where he worked. Uncle John made it possible for our whole family to be together in Portland, he gave us a house to live in when we arrived in Portland. A few years had gone by before we had another death in the family it seem if though there were an epidemic in the family with that many deaths occurring that often in the family. Cousin Fred, one of father's favorite nephews, the Korean war veteran who had been wounded in battle, they were fighting for pork chop hill when a enemy threw a hand grenade, exploding as he was trying to climb the hill, sending fragments over the area that his squad was in, he and others in his squad received injuries from the grenade. He had received an injury to his head and he wore a steel plate in his head. He passed away after many years of wearing the steel plate. He left one child, a boy and a wife behind. We all stayed together as family. When one family member passes on, another was born. The second child was born to my sister and her husband, this was another boy, sister wanted a girl this time around but, God knew best. He was given the name of Anthony, 'Tony' Spires, he was a big baby boy and had beautiful smiles, and he had many features of the Bryant Family. He had features also of his father Arthur Spires. Cousin Fred received a Military Funeral and was buried in a military cemetery.

We tried to drown all of sorrows in being more active, during hunting season, we would deer hunt, elk hunt, jack rabbit and fowl.

We usually, hunted in the months of October, and November for deer, and elk in November and a week or two in December. Eastern Oregon is one of the most beautiful places in the Nation. High desert, covered snow during the snow season, during the spring and summer months, you had many lakes and rivers to fish in. This part of Oregon is different than other parts of the State. There are wide open spaces, to hunt, fish, or just go and enjoy the scenery. These practices continue to this date. There are many more people that have joined in our ventures. We usually, have a meeting before we get ready for our hunting trip so we can get our dates and travel plans together, we take a count of how many are going and pair up the riders and the vehicle they would traveling in. All vehicles had a CB, and we all would be on the same channel, keeping in contact with one another in case of emergencies. Much fun were had talking to each other on the CB, the trip was a 6 hr. trip one way, when we arrived, the first thing we would do is to choose the same spot or location that we had the year before, then we would gather all the fire wood that we needed, after we had put our tents up and un-loaded our supplies. We carried enough supplies to last a week there was a big camp fire that night and we all sat around the camp fire enjoying each other. We sometimes, cooked our own food, and other times we would have a designated cook who would cook for ten to fifteen people, after dinner, we would hunt for a few more hours, until dark. After we had gotten our equipment put away, we would sit around the camp fire and play dominoes or cards. If some one had downed a deer, we all helped out in bringing the deer back to camp, hung the animal onto a strong tree limb and began to dress it out. Many times there were three or four deer killed, some on different days, the deer remained hanging on the limb covered with cheese cloth until the State police or Game enforcement officer made sure the animal was of legal taking. Our favorite camping area was high on top of the Long Creek mountain, elevation was seven thousand feet above sea level, surrounded by high peaks, steep cliffs, and deep canyons, when the first shots were fired on opening day, most of the animals would flee to the bottom of the canyon for safety, we had to go to the bottom of the canyon to flush them out, we hoped to run them top side so we would not have to kill one in the deep canyon. There were many animals that used the deep canyon for food and safety. Among some of the animals that lived there are bear and deer, elk, coyote, wolves and other species of animals and fowls. We had much fun being in good company with our friends and enjoying the scenery. Jack rabbit hunting usually, started in January through February and did not hunt but for one day, we would leave early in the morning, hunt all day and return back home late that same day.

Returning home from a week of deer hunting; tents were taken down, supplies loaded up, and the camping area was left as clean or better than it was when we arrived there, we took pride in keeping the area clean. However, this was a National Forest; we all had a responsibility in keeping the forest clean. After loading all of our supplies and deer tied down for the long trip back home, we would come to a small town called Long Creek, a town that had much history during the early settlement years. There had been many battles fought with Native Americans, coming down the steep high way that leads through town, you could see the old concrete block houses that serve as safe places for the settlers during raids from the Natives. The block houses had square firing and look out holes, cut out of top portion of the block houses to fire on the raiders and to protect their live stock from theft. When we entered into the town, the State Game and Patrol would check your vehicle for any out of season game or if we had our hunting license and deer tags in order. When they had finished their check, we were given the ok sign and let us continue our trip home. We made a few stops along the way back home, stopping at gas stations, eating at a specific restaurant. The people knew that this would be the time of year that they could make money on all of the hunters that would stop by their restaurant. From Arlington, or Biggs junction it was a straight three hour drive, following the Mighty Columbia all the way into Portland. This had been a safe and a most beautiful trip. Each person was dropped off at his home and his supplies, if deer was brought back; the deer was taken to a meat market where the deer was dressed and made into steaks, sausages, jerky, and roast. Meats were divided up among the hunters.

Chapter Four

We had been gone for a week and were anxious to re-fresh. We were glad to see our love ones again and they were glad to see us, preparing to go back to work. I had to spend more time with my girl friend before I went back. Mae, my girl friend had a large family, she had three sisters and five brothers, we all had began to feel comfortable with each other, they began to develop trust and cooperation in me. Her parents also had more trust in me. I always put on my best behavior when ever I was around them. Mar, would approve of me when things became a little heated between girl friend and I, this made me feel good, knowing that she would be on my side of the issue, Mar was a good person to have in those bad situations. Mae's decisions were not easily influenced by what were said. As we dated and learned more about one another, we began to understand each other better. We came to the position that when one of us would go to a party, then the other would come also. My friend Jack, and myself would not attend a party with out our girl friends. We had begun to get quite serious about each other, which in my opinion was a good thing. That meant that she wanted to be true to me also, she wanted someone that she could call a real boy friend, and I wanted a true girl friend. A few more years passed, she graduated from high school. We later became engaged to get married. We had to talk to our parents to seek their approval. Mother didn't take this too easily; she wanted me to make sure this was what we wanted to do. Father was a little more relaxed when he was told of what we wanted to do. He was a man and he went through a similar situation, he knew soon or later I would want to prove my man hood and raise a family also. I continued to work and tried to save all the money that I could.

I had to talk to her parents and tell them of our intention. I talked to her oldest brother, and informed him of what we had intended to do. He gave me his stamp of approval. We both, felt good by receiving our family's approvals. Each one of our family wished the very best for their loved ones. We had known each other for five years, and the six year we would announce our intent to get married on that particular date. She did not want a big wedding, she wanted a private wedding with few people attending, after the wedding, and we would have an open house reception. When the time came to get married, her sister, my sister, and my first cousin Robert, the brother of Fred, the Korean War veteran, traveled across the Columbia River into the State of Washington with us to get married. We became husband and wife. Coming back to Portland, our very first stop was at her parent's home. They applauded us and wished us well. They had lost a daughter and gained another son. Our next stop would be at my parents home, where we were also greeted with well wishes and applause. This will be our home for three months. We had to wait for an apartment house that we liked and we had talked to the owner about our interest in the duplex, apartment, he said that the double occupancy apartment had all up to date appliances and heating equip., also a new cooling system installed, and it needed yard work and painting done also. The apartment will be available when all off the repairs are done; he said he would" notify us when he have all off these things done to it." The last tenants have been out in a short period of time. This was a descent apartment in a nice and respectable neighborhood and close to where my parents live. Some repair work before we could move into it. A new roof, some plumbing, paint before it is made available to us and would become vacant, it was only one block from where my parents lived. Samuel, my baby brother had finished high school and about to go away to college. Mother was losing all of her children, and she and father were feeling bad about it.

Mother's Father; Passing of grandfather was a big disappointment to us all, especially, mother who took it very hard. Like all deaths, you are never ready to accept it when it comes. We knew there would be more sorrow and disappointments in the family, but no one was ready

The Long Journey

to accept it. Grandfather, the one that we used to go live with on the farm had passed away. All the fun that the Cousins had when we all met there on the farm to spend summer vacations, the things he taught us about farming and all the farm animals. All these memories and many more he left behind for us to cherish forever. Grandmother would be without her long time husband, his children without their father and to see Grandmother in sorrow. Mother left Portland, going to the farm in Wesson, Mississippi to be with her sisters and her brother and to attend the funeral service and burial, they spent time with Grandmother trying to keep her talking and offering her assurance. Mother however, did have an older brother that lived on the property with his family, and her baby sister lived in the same house with Grandmother. She would have family close by to help her with most of the chores on the farm. Some crops would not be planted, just the necessary ones for food. Some live stock had to be sold off. Mother had been gone for three weeks and was returning to Portland, this was her first air flight. She flew from Portland to Mississippi and back to Portland on her first travel by air. Mother arrived in Portland the same day that she left Mississippi. Only a few hours by plane compared to a few days by train. By train, the trip was longer, but she saw beautiful snow covered mountain peaks from the plane; she also arrived to her destination in a fraction of the time.

Arrived at the Portland International Air Port; Father and I picked mother up from air port and came home, she arrived on a Saturday Evening. Brother Samuel was leaving for college in Boise, Idaho and would leave on Monday. Mother would have time to see him before he left for school. We would be moving into our apartment house soon. We would only be a block away from where my parents lived. Wife had put furniture on a lay a way plan until we were ready to move in. We received a call from the owner, telling us that both, apartments in the duplex were for rent or lease, wife notified her oldest sister who lived in Klamath Falls, Oregon, that the apartment next to where we would be living is available also. Her and her husband was interested in the apartment. They came up from Klamath Falls on that week end and secured the deposit on it. They had to go back to pack, and to make preparation to move to Portland. My wife and I moved into the apartment a week before they did, we were situated in our apartment when they arrived. Her husband had been promised a job here when he came here to live. My wife liked the idea of her sister living next door to us. We all lived in that apartment for one year. Her sister and husband purchased a home one block from where we were living in the apartment. They had purchased a beautiful home. Wife and I lived in the apartment for another year before we purchased a house in north Portland. We moved in the house which was directly in front of a beautiful park, it had a beautiful rose garden, swimming, basketball court and more athletic activities. We had been married more than one year, now was the time to start our family. My first born was a beautiful girl, who looked a little like her mother and she had some of the features of the Bryant's side of the family. Wife's oldest sister named her. Michele Denise was the name she gave her. Artelia, her oldest sister had a baby girl also. There were no boys in the first two that were born. Although we wanted the first born to be a boy were completely satisfied with a girl, she was healthy and beautiful. Mother and father loved her, sister admired her also. A few months earlier, sister had her third child, another girl to the family, this had been what she had wanted, a girl in her family of two boys. We had begun to make up the numbers in our family after many deaths had occurred, sorrow became happiness. I had started to work a part-time job to help with expensive; I worked as a security patrol officer for the new shopping center that were built. Lloyd Center, this was a beautiful center, it had nearly every thing that you would want. It had many restaurants, theaters, and more.

I worked the night shift, and still had my day job at the steel foundry. More money was coming in to help with bills and other expensive. I worked the part-time job for three years, after two years with the first born, wife became pregnant again. Second time was another girl, wife's mother named this one, she named her Joyce Marie, she was another beautiful baby, and she had even more features of the Bryant's side of the family. The saying is," you could always tell if you were related to the Bryant's by the big round face and the smiles

The Long Journey

that they have". She had all of this, round face, beautiful smile. Even when she cried she was beautiful. Now I had become a father twice over. I liked the father hood role, it was inspiring and rewarding. I had seen my father raise us from birth to where we were at that time, I knew some of the obstacles that you would have to over come, and this was a challenge to see how my man hood had developed Putting food on the table, paying for house hold expensive and other out side expensive. Some time going to work when your body was not feeling like doing it. All these things I had seen my father endure. I wanted to be as good of a family provider as he had been for us. If there ever was a hero to choose, my father would be the one. He taught me the difference between male and man; the responsibilities of a man and father, a real man take care of his responsibilities and will not slack on them. If I could be half the man that he was, then I would feel if though I had accomplished much. Time was coming when I had to leave for summer camp. We would be traveling by truck convoy to Fort Lewis, Washington for our two weeks of National Guard training, we had to take all of our field gear with us in deuce and a half military trucks. Many trucks, jeeps, and tractor trailers, all loaded with our field supplies, we travel north on interstate five with Military and State Police escort all way to Fort Lewis, Washington.

Arriving at Fort Lewis; we pitched all tents, kitchen tent where they would cook and eat hot meals, huge squad size tent for sleeping a squad of thirteen. Summer camp, we lived mostly in the field, we cooked and ate rations and hot food in the field. I was a member of the 41st, infantry division, 162nd, regiment. The unit had much history during the Korean War. We cut trees down and built bridges to cross a body of water or a deep ravine. The bridge had to support a deuce and a half truck loaded. After the vehicles had passed over, then we would place explosives at certain spots on the bridge structure to blow it up. There were no mistakes made, we could not afford to make any, one mistake and we all could have been blown up. On the week end we had the liberty to go any place we chose as long as we were back for roll call on Monday morning. Many came back to Portland and others went to Seattle or Tacoma to spend their week end, other guards came back to Portland to spend time with their families. My family was proud to see me back for the week end; things were going well with the family. Mother had received a letter from my brother Samuel, and he was doing well in Idaho his schooling were doing well and he would be home for his summer vacation. I had one week left on my active duty training at Fort Lewis and I would be home for another year, until the next summer camp that would start in April. Friends and I drove back to camp to finish our last week of training, we made a few stops along the way back and enjoyed the scenery and made rest stops. When we arrived, on the same day that we left Portland, we began to check in and let the authorities know that we had come back on base. Then we prepared for the last week ahead. When training were over, we loaded all of our supplies aboard the trucks secured them and headed back to Portland, the convoy required Military and state police escort back to our Head Quarters in Portland. Vehicles had to be un-loaded fueled up and taken back to the motor pool. Then we would be free to call our love ones to come and pick us up. My unit was based at the Portland Air Base. My wife and my two young daughters came to pick me up, now we are together again until next summer. Our parents were notified of my arrival and all went well on the return trip back home.

Monday morning; returning to work, co workers were glad to see me return. Many questions were asked on my training adventure, they knew what the policy of the company was and they understood that you had an obligation to go to training camp each year. When duty calls, they have to let you go without any penalty. These policies were from both, Federal and State Government. I went back to full time and part time jobs that I had before I left for camp. Working two jobs, I had less time to socialize at night, the part time job called for Friday and Saturday nights work, some holidays. I worked this security patrol for two years and then was hired by the Wacky- in -hut security firm; they had the contract of providing the security for the Portland Memorial Coliseum. There were many activities taking place daily and nightly at the Coliseum. Portland had put a first- time professional Basketball team together, and we had to provide security for the games and other events, pay was better and working more hours per week. I had the opportunity of meeting many of the athletes, players such as: Wilt, Petrie, Clyde, and Lloyd Neal. There were many more that I met. We worked many nationally known concerts. There was enough work to keep us busy the year round. We were paid a minimum of four hours even though most of the time we worked much less than four hours. This was a good job and I worked there for a longer period of time.

Another member added to the family: Sister had added another member to her family, only this time it was a girl. This is what they had been hoping for, having a girl in the family. She was a beautiful girl and had the features of her mom and her father, she was given the name of Catherine, this was a pretty name to fit a beautiful baby girl, and she had already become the pride of her family, her two boys having a sister and mom having a daughter. This is what they had wanted and they received a beautiful gift from God. Everyone had joy to see sister and family welcome a new baby girl. My parents were pleased to have another granddaughter and grandchild added to the family. We were gradually, adding to the family. The family was Church going and God believing people, and that any thing that you would pray to God for and if he saw a need for you to have it, at his own time and choosing you would receive it. Prayer and patient is the key 'to an answer. I have seen many Prayers answered from God, my parents' consistent prayers; many times I was a recipient of my parents praying to God on my behalf. I know that my family was a God fearing, God trusting family. If a family ventured too far to the left of what was expected of them, then prayer would bring them back to where they are supposed to have been. The teaching and proper raising of us were not in vain, God answers prayer, I can attest to that many times over. I had been praying to God for a son, he had already given me two beautiful girls, and now at his time and choosing for him to bless me with a son, all I needed to do was to be patient and wait on God.

Grandmother passes away: it seem to be holding true, that one come into the family, and another passes on. This has been the trend in our family for many years, we all were so proud of sister having a new baby girl and enjoying the time that she was born, and adding to the family, these were happy times. Now the sorrow times are back. Mother has lost both, parents. Her father was the first to pass away, and now her mother is gone. As hard as it is to see them leave us, we have no doubt where they went. We know beyond a doubt, that they lived the way that God wanted them to live. The big lost is to the people that knew them and her family. We know that we will not see her again in this life, but our hopes that we will come together some day. Mother left for Mississippi to attend the funeral and burial. This was hard on mother, happy for a birth in the family but, sorrow for the death of her mother. She would have a chance to talk to her other sisters and her brother, now grandmother is gone they would have to come together to see what they agree to do with the property and rest of the live stock. They made an agreement and carried out grandmother's wishes. Uncle Emanuel remained living on the property as he and his family had always done. Aunt Alberta remained in the house that she always lived in, living with grandmother and grandfather. Some of the land was sold off. The mineral rights were not sold. Mother did what she had to do and returned back to Portland. Sad occasion to have to go to, but happy to come back home, we always came together once a month for bible study and major holidays, we would have studies of the events that took place in biblical times and what was expected of us in the present time.

Dinner was always over to our parent's home on Christmas, Easter, and thanks giving day. We had some good friends to participate in Christmas dinners and some Bible classes. We stayed true to the Church that we chose to be our home and family church. Reverend Wendell Wallace was our beloved Pastorate. He was nationally known and well respected.

We started to attend his church when Aunt Oral, mother's twin sister told her about the Pastor and his church. Mother had been looking for a church that she could relate to. She wanted the right type of gospel, singing, preaching, and the right attitude of the congregation. She wanted a God filled Pastor who would not shun the truth about our salvation. She had been raised as a faithful servant and she wanted to be sure to attend that type of church, she also wanted her children and grandchildren to be exposed to this type of Gospel. Father wanted the same thing that mother wanted for himself and his children and grand children, he was less vocal than mother but every bit of dedicated to Christ and the Good works. We as a family have been attending this Church to this day. Leader- ship has change and some members have passed on and gone to other churches, the majority of the church members still exist. Younger members of the family were all dedicated and Baptized at this church. The name of the church has changed. The traditions have remained, and many people from other areas have joined since that time. New members are coming in all the time.

Ocean fishing: going fishing in the Pacific Ocean is one of the most enjoyable experiences a person could ever have. The big blue body of water is one of the great wonders of this planet, the constant roar of the waves, the swells of the water, low tides, high tides, storms and how the winds suddenly come up. All of this is in order. When you see all of the magnificent natural work, you know that man could not have done this. The sea animals, huge fish, whale, shark, even the sea fowl do what they were created to do. We sometimes charter a fishing boat and go out to sea five or ten miles, sometime the ocean out that far is completely different then close to the shore, as deep as it is, the water is sometime calm, other times it is so rough that you wonder if you would get back to shore. We usually, catch huge fish out this far in the ocean, occasionally shark. Most common fish that we catch is huge cod, salmon, sea bass, ocean perch and other fish. Being out to sea this far is a sure thing that what ever you catch will be huge. Many times when we ocean fish, we would fish off the long jetty, big rocks that were put in place by the Army Engineers to break the high waves and high tides, trying to slow the waves down keeping the low lying areas from flooding out. These huge rocks serve as a feeding ground for many of the ocean's species of fish. We catch perch of all species, cod of many species and other fish. This is a good place to lay back and relax, sitting on the huge rocks and listen to the waves pound the big rocks, occasionally, seeing a ship traveling far out into the sea.

In this type of setting ,enjoyment is there even though you might not limit out on your fish, coming back home through the burned area of the 1950's where a fire burned many thousands of acres of timber. The beautiful mountain passes that wind down to the ocean. We usually, stop two or three times to smell the fresh mountain air and to observe the high mountain peaks. All this make Oregon truly, one of the most beautiful States in the union. When we arrived home, there would be a fish fry, and all the family came to my parent's home to enjoy the feast. We talked about how far that we had come and to remember how we came to Oregon. This has been a long journey for us all, we had been blessed. We never forgot our relatives that had passed away before us. We talked about our seasonal hunting trip, when did it start, and supplies that we would need for a week, contacting other hunters to start getting things together, although it would be four to five months before we actually would leave. We sat around and mother would play her piano and we all joined in to sing a song that we all knew and mother loved:" Amazing Grace, this was one of her favorite songs" When we finish, we began to go back to our own homes and prepare for Sunday's Service, some would go to Sunday school and stay for Sunday Services. Prepare for work on Monday morning. After my regular day job, I had to come home and prepare for my security job at night, at the memorial coliseum. Now that I am a family man and working most of the week, I had little time to talk to or spend time with my friend Jack. He and his girl friend had decided to become engaged and they had planned to get married in the near future.

He said he had to save money so he could buy furniture; he wanted to put things on a lay a way plan and pay as he goes. I took a couple of nights off my part time job so him and his girl friend, wife and I could go to the movies and enjoy ourselves before he got married. We gave them a stamp of approval, and said we would be in their corner. We had gone to school together, worked together and double dated together. We had been friends ever since we came to Portland, and now we have become or will become married friends. I had persuaded Jack to join the National Guard with me and finish his military obligation in Army national guards. Six months of being engaged, Jack finally, got married and moved into an apartment, he said they would live in the apartment until they had saved enough money to purchase a house. Both worked and it would not take long to save for the down payment on a house. Time came for our usual group to go deer hunting. We usually, go to Long Creek, a small town in the eastern part of Oregon, and make camp on long creek mountain, six thousand foot elevation where we could see for miles, over the canyons, prairies, and the beautiful mountain range. We did the usual thing when we arrived to the camp site. We cleared the area where we would pitch our tents and then we would un- load our supplies, gathered fire wood. We fixed dinner and sat around the camp fire telling jokes. On Saturday morning, we were geared up and ready to hunt deer. We would split up into three groups; each group would go in a different direction with a two- way radio. We wanted to stay in touch with each group just in case of an emergency. When a deer was down and they needed help to retrieve it, we would find the location of where they were and go to that location to help. Our way of doing this, have been the best way to do things. Arriving back to camp, we hung the animal from a limb and dressed it out. Games, The same procedures were done each time we went hunting and left to come home. We had to come down this long highway into town; there we would be checked for the type of game that we had killed and to check our hunting license. The State Police or State game officer would check you and if all were in order they would let you continue our trip home, some time we would use a different route to come home. We would come through the Mount Hood national forest on interstate 26, this was a beautiful scenic route, and we could see the majestic 11,000, Foot Mountain with all its snow and snow skiers. We turn off 26 after we had gotten through Mount Hood and on to interstate #80, along side of the Columbia River; this was also a beautiful scenic route it brought us into Portland. We all arrived home safe. This was our time of year to come together and go hunting, the trip there and back were intriguing. As usual, if we had meat to have processed out, the meat was divided among all members of the hunting party. Our families were glad to see us and to know that we enjoyed our hunting trip. Henry, father's younger brother, some times made sausages out of the meat that he received. I have gone hunting with he and father at night, on one of the islands in north Multnomah County and hunted for raccoons and other small animals. A carbon head light had to be used to see the animals' eyes high in the trees. We sometimes brought home three or four animals that we grounded into sausages. They were old country boys from on the farms of Mississippi, and they knew how to hunt, back then, they had to put food on the table because there were many mouths to feed. Hunting is in our blood and we enjoy it very much. One year we were stalked by a bear. A deer had been shot and down, a bear scented the killed and tried to beat us to the downed animal. We tried to locate where the deer had fallen and were looking for it, the bear was also looking for an easy meal. We met the bear coming to the same location that we were headed to, we all were afraid of each other, Mr. Banks and brother in law, Arthur Spires, shot the bear in the chest with a 306, caliber rifle, but the bear kept coming. Mr. Banks, then shot the bear in the fore head with a 300, weather b. magnum rifle that stopped the bear in his tracks, the bear lay where he fell. We waited for a few minutes to make sure the bear was dead and would not cause any harm to any of us before we started to bring him back to camp. There we dressed him out, and brought the hide to a specialist who made the hide into a throw -rug. Eddie, one of our fellow hunters, has the rug to this day.

Prayers answered: I received the good news from the wife that she was in family way again. I was glad but wondered if this would be the boy that we all had hoped some day would come. The baby was born and gladly, it was a healthy baby boy. This is what I had asked God to give to us; God did answer my prayer and gave me and the family a son and a brother to the two daughters. Mother and father were also glad. Sister knew we had wanted a boy for my next child, she also was glad for the family. She now had two boys and one girl. I had just the opposite, one boy and two girls. Sister next two children were boys; she had wanted a girl play mate with her only daughter. Their next child would be named Jar-real and her last child was a boy also, named, Byron. This made up her family of 5 children, 4 boys and one girl. As time went on I had another addition to my family, this time was another girl, and this gave us three girls and the one boy. Wife's mother named the only boy Michael D., and the last girl Carla L. The family loved all the children. Our parents like all grandparents, wanted the grandchildren to come to her house and spend more time with her and father. There were no children at home, all had gone away, either to school or started their own families, mother and father, and they were getting old and lonely. We tried to spend time at their home and time at my wife's parent's home. They all wanted to be around their grandchildren. All of the wife's sisters and brothers liked their nieces and nephew. On Holidays, we had to be sure we divided our time between the two different grandparents. If we had dinner at one of the parent's home, we had to save enough time and room in our stomachs to eat something at the other parent's home also. After dinner we sometimes took a ride out to the international air port and watch the air planes take off and land. The children like to see the big planes land and take off. I had traded my Chevy off and purchased a ford station wagon, the wagon had much room for the children to sleep and play. We would take trips to the Pacific Ocean beaches and enjoy the scenery. Many times we used a different route to come home using highway 101, north. Following the ocean up to Astoria, where the Columbia meets the ocean, this was a beautiful thing to see, after many miles to travel, it dumps into the ocean. We then used high way 30, to bring us back to Portland.

Children were growing up; we would come together and plan a camping trip with other family members. I purchased a second vehicle, this time it was a pickup truck with an 8 foot camper already mounted on it, this was the ideal thing to have for camping. The wife would not sleep in a tent, she did not trust all off the little animals that would be out at night looking for food. The truck was a ford 4x4 3/4 ton, with a 5 speed standard transmission; it also had a 360 v-8 engine, more than enough power to carry the load that we would have. We often camped in southern Oregon, on two of the most beautiful lakes in Oregon. The lakes were very deep and wide, many species of fish were in the lakes, we caught crappie, ring tail, and trout, and there were cat fish, blue gill and other perch. These lakes were all fresh water lakes that were just across the high way from the ocean. We would spend four to five days there camping out and having a fish fry. Other times we went fishing, up to the eastern part of Oregon, going through the mount hood national forest to the east side of mount hood, this terrain was completely different than the western part of the State. This terrain was all high desert with hardly any large trees; it looked like the surface of the moon. Miles upon miles of open desert land, Native American reservations and State lands. We would go to the Hay stack dam and lake where we would set up camp. Both, small and big mouth bass were in this lake, along with perch, cat fish and trout. This time of year, the heat was very hot, and some time it got windy. We were high above sea level and received the winds from the pacific and the mountain. Returning home we used the same route, coming through the Mount Hood national forest. The scenery was beautiful, the thick, tall trees of the national forest, the beautiful snow capped mountain peak. We all had an enjoyable time. We arrived home safely, and called wife's parents and let them know that we were back in town. Preparing for the next week's work, I had to go to bed early so I could be up early to start my day job. Then I would come home, shower and eat dinner. Then I would prepare to go to my part time security job, three hours or more on the part time job. Many times I had to sit up and talk to the wife about what had taken place on that night, basketball or a major concert.

Samuel; baby brother had finished his schooling in Idaho, and was back home with our parents. They were glad that he had come back home. He had searched for a job and a radio station gave him a job in advertisement, he traveled all over the state of Oregon. He said he liked the job and that he had seen much of the State. Samuel joined the Army reserve, this way he beat the draft. He had to leave for six months training, he went to the same fort that I had taken my training at. Fort Ord, California. He had been doing well and they appointed him to a squad leader's position, this was an acting position where he would train under the squad leader's guidance. Samuel was a model solider for his platoon and his company. The army wanted him to join up with the regular army and become a regular active duty solider, "he said that he thought long and hard", but decided not to do it on the last day of his six months obligation. He returned home when he had finished his training and met a very pretty young lady, he introduced her to his family. Her name was Rose Dean, her parents were well known in the Black community, and their family had much credibility in the Portland area. Her parents own and operated a barber and beauty shop in the same building. Her mother ran the beauty parlor, and he ran the barber shop. My family liked Rose, she was respectable and knowledgeable, and her parents had been in Portland for many years before my family came. Everyone in the black areas knew them and many went to their shop for their services. Samuel was seeing her on a steady basis and he was getting serious about her.

My parents knew that he was getting serious and it would be a matter of time before he would be asking her hand in marriage. Two years passed, and Samuel told my parents what his intentions were, he went through the usual things with parents, asking if he is sure this is what he wanted to do, and the high and low things in marriage. He assured my parents that this is what he and she wanted to do. After talking to him he remained consistent in what he wanted to do and then mother and father gave him their Blessing. In the near future, he would announce the time and date soon. He had yet to choose a place. He said the Church that we attended would be more likely. The word was out, people that knew them both, were notified and a date were set, short time later, and he would announce the place of the wedding. Samuel was the last of the children that would leave home to start his own family. We were all excited, and help them in any way that we could. They had saved for furniture for their apartment, and other expensive. Rose worked for the air line; she worked there for many years even when she was in high school she worked part time. After graduating from school, she went full time for the air line and stayed there until she retired. Samuel was still at the radio station, but now he preferred to stay close around home. He had to seek employment else where. The date came and the marriage would take place as planned, they would have the wedding at the church that the family attends. The Metropolitan Church of God in Christ, this is the same Church that we found to be our home church, the name and location have changed but the tradition is the same. The wedding was a beautiful wedding, people from all around attended, some of her co-workers, and people that her parents knew who lawyers, Drs., were and other well known people in the city. They got married and had a reception after the wedding. We became sociable and met her family. We all wished them well. A few months went by and Samuel wanted to go fishing with the usual party of fishermen, he always liked to fish but he did not like to hunt. It takes too much patience to hunt for, or wait until a deer jump up. He did like camping out with the campers sitting around the camp fire, eating and playing dominoes. Grandchildren were growing up and had started school, some were in pre-school and some went to grade school. They all like the outdoors.

Wife started working part-time for a day care center; she would be off work before the children were out off school. She earned extra money to purchase some of the things that she and the children wanted. She truly, had a way with children; all the children and staff liked her very much and depended on her to run the day care on a part-time basic. "She told them, she would help out as much as she could help, but that she had other obligations". We had children that she had to pick up from school and didn't want any extra time added on to her schedule. The school that the children attended was 10 blocks away from where we lived and we did not want them to walk home from school at that time. Usually, she would be off work and at school to pick them up before school was out. When arriving home the wife had a full schedule in getting the children settled down and changing their school clothing, preparing dinner, washing clothes and many more chores. She truly had her day full. She cared very much on how the children were dressed when they went to school and out into the public. We made sure they were obedient to their teachers and other adults. We received from many people on how well behaved the children were, this made us feel happy, believing that we were on the right track in trying to raise a young family. Wife worked at the day care center for 4 years, then she let the job go, she was better served at home, taking care of the things that a mother and wife should do in raising a family. When I arrived home from work, the wife had dinner nearly ready and the children in the back yard playing. She made sure that they would not leave the yard and be out of sight. She was a good wife and a good mother.

Chapter Five

Excited and happy to see him start his family, his first child was a healthy boy. He was very much pleased to have his first child a boy. His wife's family was overjoyed to have a grandson. Looking back on our lives growing up, we didn't see our baby brother growing up and starting his family. He was so young at the time and I thought at the time that he would be with my parents forever, however, he was the baby of our family and my parents loved their baby boy. Like people that have gone before us, they too take the giant step in to the unknown, but hoping thing would turn out the way you had dreamed off. There are 10 grandchildren in our family, four girls and six boys. These births to the family, had replaced the numbers of deaths that had taken place in the family. This is the way of God. One leaf falls off the tree and a new one takes it place. This thing death has been around as long as life and everything that breathe is going to die, soon or later. We are never ready to accept it when it comes; each time it happens it is a new adjustment. I suppose it is the sure mystery of it all. We were proud to see God was giving us new members to our family. As the baby boy grew, Samuel would take him with the men of the family to fishing, he liked it very much and as he grew more, he would camp out with us and enjoy the natural things in the wild. I am not sure who named the baby boy by the name of Reggie, it really did not matter who named him, he was part of the Bryant's and that was the only thing that did matter. My father who pleasured having his grandchildren around him on the week end, used to sit the youngest children on his knee and talk to them and give them candy or chewing gum. Friday nights and Saturday father used to have his happy hours. He was a controlled drinker, mostly alcohol, and some times he drank beer. Mother did not like for him to drink any type of alcoholic beverages. Father worked hard all of his life and this was his way of relaxing, this gave him courage to talk more and be more cheerful. He never missed a day of work because of any alcoholic problem, he only drank on the week end and that wasn't every week end. Monday morning, he always was up and ready to go to work. During the winter months, some times we got much snow, too much for him to drive to work, so he would leave home two hours earlier than usual and walk to work. His route there was across the Broadway Bridge and into the North West Portland industrial area; this is where his job was located. He only walked to work when the roads were too slippery to take a chance on driving. His return trip home, he also walked. No more than twice in one week did he have to walk; most of the roads would be cleared within that time. Father knew what it took to be a provider and a complete family man. He was shown the way at an early age.

Later, father's age and hard work began to catch up with him, he suffered a minimum stroke, he became hospitalized for two weeks and the stroke left him with a minor deformity of his bottom lip, it did not look bad but if you knew him like his family and friends did, then you could detect a small deformation of his bottom lip. After two weeks of being home, father became restless and wanted to return back to work. The company gave him the option of coming back to work when ever he felt up to coming back. Father did return to work and worked there for many more years. Father had to make changes in his life style, he had to eliminate his happy hours on the week end, watch his salt intake and various other things he had to change. It was not easy for someone that had many happy hours through out his life. This all started in Wesson, Mississippi with the enjoyment after working in the fields all week, this is when all of his friends and relatives came together and enjoyed each other's company. This was a tradition for them to come together after a week's hard work behind the plows of horses and mules. This was the only way they knew how to blow off steam. At that time, people of the Deep South did not have much money to purchase alcohol so they brewed their own alcohol

The Long Journey

with corn, potatoes, sugar cane and what ever else they used to make the spirits. I believe that God saw that these were well meaning good men that did not abuse alcohol but used it to stimulate their attitudes, mental out look on the situation at that time. There were many things that they were thankful unto God for, he had done for them and their families. God had brought him out of the land of Mississippi and into a new land where he prospered. He had raised his children in a new land and watched his children grow and start their own families, now time was coming to an end in this life, he grew older and health had begun to fail him. He had done what God had expected of him in bringing his family out of bondage in Mississippi. The way out had already been made for him to do so.

Mother being a dedicated Christian always prayed to God for our support. She had come from a God fearing family and looked to God for her needs and her desires. She had come from a long way to where she was; she gave thanks to God for her family, her home that he had shown her in a dream. Her faith in God never dwindled, her faith was steadfast. We all looked up to mother for much advice. When we had a problem in life, we prayed about it and told mother so that she would pray also. We also knew that a mother's prayer would be answered. These prayers gave us confident in the power of prayer. Mother was growing old also and she had seen her children escape from Mississippi and start a new life in a new land. She watched her children grow up and have families of their own, with her testimony, no one couldn't tell her that prayer doesn't count. She was living evidence. Mother gained a reputation for praying for people that needed prayer, everyone on the long street where she lived, knew she was a praying woman. I know that we humans all make mistakes and sin one way or another, but the truth is, I never saw mother do anything or heard her say anything that were not pleasing in God's sight. Her travel was very limited, she would go to church every Sunday and when she went to the grocery store or visit the good will stores, she would come home. We would sometime come by her house and bring her out to our house to spend some time. She needed to leave home and get out and visit other people. Mother would read the Bible and play the piano, father was at work and she and God were the only ones that were in the house. She sang old songs, and played old songs on her piano. The songs were back when she was a child and they sang those songs in church. "Thought how far she had come, from the fields on the farm to Jackson and out to Portland, Oregon". God had shown her the very house that she and her family would own. Songs that she sang were all about these things. Father might have been the bread winner and provider, but mother was the spiritual leader of her family. Another member was about to be added to the Bryant's family. Samuel and wife received a new baby boy to his family; this would be his second child and his second boy. We now have seven boys in the family and four girls. Parent's now have eleven grandchildren. She thanked God that she was able to see them. The newest member to the family was named; Emmy L. We welcomed the new baby boy and celebrated them on the new born.

Wife's sister, Mar, had met a friend from Jackson, Mississippi. He was here to make a better life for him self. Arthur had known him since they went to the same high school and lived only one block from each other, they have known each other's family for years. Arthur's younger brother and Gray were in the same classes at the high school, so they were the best off friends. Arthur's brother had come out six months earlier to seek the same thing as all of us did. They both received jobs at the steel foundry in different departments. Mar, and Gray liked each other very much, and after a while they would become husband and wife. Arthur's brother, he also found his love and would become husband and wife. They eventually, moved into an apartment that was a few blocks from each other. Mar, was working and Billie Ruth Mack worked also. Both, marriages saved enough money in about two years to purchase each a home. Mar and her husband purchased a home on the next street behind us, directly behind us. Only a concreted alley way separated their home from our home. This is where they live to this day. Billie Ruth and her husband purchased a home about ten blocks away from us. This was a good thing for my wife and her sister; they were very close and constantly stayed in touch with one another, either by phone or crossing the alley to each other's house. Mar Had a baby girl later in that year and they all were pleased to have their first child. They named her Deidre, Jim Grey, Mar Husband, also worked part-time for the same security and at the same location that I did, at the memorial coliseum. We both went to work together and came home together. This was a perfect set up for all of us. Both, wives had a baby sitter if they needed one. Billie Ruth had her first child and it was a baby boy. She and her family were also proud to have an addition to their family. We all are close friends and relatives to this day, our spirit seem to be the one most unifying force.

States were bad for us, but Mississippi was the worst of them all, the reasons for being like this were; no justice, low wages and the enforcement of strict racial segregation. Unresolved murders, people missing and the murders never brought to justice. We all hoped that one day we would see things change, that there would be justice and that people would not be jailed for a longer period of time for the same crime as white people had and still is committing. This was a Jim Crow State and they did not have any shame about them. This kind of law had been going on for four hundred years. Some things may be getting better, but there is still a long ways to go for justice under the law. I could not understand until this day, why would those white people in the south use the religion of Christian. I don't believe that they know the definition of the word Christian. They either don't know or they don't care. Their way of life is everything but, Christ like. They can treat their brothers any way they choose, discriminate and do nearly, everything that the Bible says not to do. If these people truly believe in God, then they would try to live as close to his Commandments as they could. It's my belief that they don't believe what they are teaching and preaching. The whole world can see their un-Christian like ways. The only thing that I miss about this State is the relatives and friends that were left behind. I know in God's own time, things will change and it will be a new day in the south for Black people. I was a young boy when I left Mississippi and had not been back in forty-five years. It wasn't until Brother Samuel, and first cousins came together to have a family re-union. They put it all together and it was a huge success. From that time on we have had a family re-union in different States every other year. Each time we have the re-union, more and more of our Relatives attend. There were relatives that I never seen before and some that had been a very long time. If Brother Samuel, and cousins had not come together to make this re-union possible, I don't know if we would have ever had a coming together of relatives in such large numbers. Many said that the only thing that would keep them from ever attending any of the re-unions would be sickness or death. This is the best thing that ever happened to them, seeing all your relatives coming together at one place, the re-unions are well organized, many volunteers helping to continue the turn out and the successes that have been positive.

My family was growing up and they wanted to know more about their roots. It is hard to tell them where you came from and how we came out west. They wanted to know more about the ancestors of the past. Where did they come from and who were their parents. It was a hard thing to tell them that most Blacks can only go back in history four or five generations. And up to that point we all had come from the Continent of Africa. We came to these shores as slaves, sold and worked as animals by the so called Christians. Mississippi was the last State in the union that would keep their property and continue to dehumanize Blacks in their State. It had the worst of all the southern states for human rights violations. It wasn't until the federal laws were passed and enforced to some extent, the rights for Blacks to vote and slowly enter into citizenship. I am convinced; racism is through out these United States. Mississippi may be the worst State in the union, but it is not the only State that fit that mold. As beautiful as Oregon is there is much racism in many of the small rural areas. There used to be a law that would not let Blacks move in or purchase any land in the State. When they did eventually, allow Blacks to live and purchase property in the State, mostly in Portland, where most Blacks live, they had certain areas that they could live or purchase a house in. We were fortunate when we moved to Oregon, things were changing, if you had enough money they would sell you a house in the more up- scale areas. It is good to see things making a change. Many of the people still have that racist view, and they will go to their graves with their views. I am confident that when the older people pass on, things will continue to get better for Blacks. As most young people continue to go to school together and intermingle together, things will change. The lies that were told on Blacks and other minorities about being inferior were being found out to be just that, a lie. Younger whites had begun to see the lies that their ancestors had told them. However, they were Christian, and if you are a Christian, then you would do what pleases God. It will come a day when things get much better; we will have less discrimination and more justice under the law.

I often wondered why one group of people think that they are the only people that God created, and everyone else just happen to pop up? This big wide world was created for all of God's creatures; he gave us everything we would need here on this earth, all our food plants, meats to eat, fish to eat, and fruits of all assortments. We were supposed to live together on Earth, and become good stewards over what God had given us. He gave us a free will to choose and make decisions. He also gave us the law to live by, and the consequences of choosing the wrong way. For some reason, man chose the wrong way to live and now we will suffer the consequences of what we have done. I don't agree with some scientists, when they "say we just happened, that we evolved from some other species of animal form". Only a fool would say this. There is too much evidence around us to not think there is a more Superior power some where in the universe than man. We see the stars, the moon, planets that we can see, and many more that we cannot see. We see life and death on a daily basis; we see the good, the bad and the ugly things of man. God created all of it and without him there were nothing created. He knew that humans would be challenged with all of this. He gave us a way out of the evils of life through serving him and keeping his commandments. When we sin God sends a correction consequence and man should realize that someone, some where had violated his law. He said that the" sun shines on the just and the un-just, the rain falls on the just and the un-just. His blessings also come upon the just and un-just." He is not an un-just God, anyone violates his Holy Law will suffer consequences. However, he did give us a way out of our sins. We ask him to" forgive us and repent from our evil ways. This is the only re-course that man has to be in good standings with him." We were created to serve God and to bring joy and satisfaction to him, and when we don't measure up to expectations, then things will happen to you. You would become un-productive and not in his will how you should live your life here on earth. Father had passed on with a massive heart attack. He had suffered a minor stroke a few years earlier, but re- gained his strength and continued to work and continued to carry on as usual on a limited basis. I was at work when it happened. I received a message from my supervisor that for me to come home quickly, I did just that, when I arrived at his home, mother was at the top of the stairs weeping over her long time husband and friend. The emergency persons had arrived and tried to revive him but could not. They told mother that it was one of those rare heart attacks, when it come upon you, there would hardly be any time to do anything. I know that we all will leave one day with something to take us out, but each time it comes we can never be ready to accept it. It's the ones you leave behind is the ones that do the suffering, refusing to let go of your love one. Whether they are Christian or sinner, when your time is up on this earth, you will have to go. There will be no canceling of your appointment; each person should try to be ready when it comes, because he said you know not the day or the hour when he will call us in from the battle field. My father was the only real hero in my life. He was a strong man, both, mentally and spiritually. He endured the worst things that men can do to other men. The man that I knew worked hard to feed his family and to make sure that their lives would be better than the life that he had lived growing up. He took us away from one place to another so that would give us a better chance at life. He also was a loving husband to mother. It hurt to this date to think about him, the things that he taught us growing up. We learned about soul salvation, praise and worship and to always put God first before we attempted to make any hard decisions. Wait on him for the answer. It might not come when we want it to come, but in his time you will receive an answer, one way or another. You might not like the answer that he will reveal to you, but he will let you know the reason why the request was not answered. After a while, you will begin to see the reason you were denied or rejected. Usually, if you insist on having it your way and not his way there are consequences to suffer. Father was always there for us to talk to about things in life's hassle passing the torch; this is what life is all about. Each generation hopefully, advances spiritually, earthly and in all phases of our life. The torch was passed during the civil rights movement. Each group that was chosen to carry out the mission of civil rights only went so far. Then God would rise up others to run the other part of the relay. So the race continues to this date. In due time, we will come to our destination in life. Patience and obedient is the key to running this race, the race of life. The fuel that we need to run the race is the knowledge of the word of God, having knowledge of the word of God in running this race, you may become tired, you may want to give up and say what is the use of trying to run this race, you might be knocked down, but you will jump back up and continue the race, there are no quitters in this race. Knowing that in the end, a great reward awaits those that finishes. When you have seen God work in people's lives then you can say, there is a God. I say this because of the" experiences that I have had in him". He came to my rescue on many occasions; this is why I can say with "certainty that God is alive and he works in the lives of men". In life's journey, father had been knocked down many times but he never stayed there. He immediately, got back up and continued the journey of life. He knew how to suffer. He knew what it was to try to achieve things for his family. The life he had when he was growing up did not even afford a way out of his situation. There were many members of his family and each member contributed to the survival of the family as a whole. From his oldest brother to his youngest, they all had to do something to sustain their life on the farm. They plowed fields, harvested the crops, cut wood to sell to the mill and much more to survive. Doing without the finer things of life, was no problem for him, however, he did have dreams of some day, and he would accomplish some of things he had hoped to achieve. My hero had been a" trail blazer for my life". He had done what was expected of a father for his family. Mother knew she had married a good man and that he was a good father to her children. Now father is gone and it would be a hard adjustment for mother to cope with. He left behind four children and eleven grandchildren. Hopefully, we all will come together one day. Changing jobs; one year after father passed away, I left my day job at the steel foundry, and worked full time on my security part-time job that I had. There were too many memories at the steel foundry for me to continue working there. I had worked fifteen years at the company and probably would have worked more if father had not passed. He had been the one that was instrumental in me getting the job and I did not want to let him down by quitting. I had thought of other things that I wanted to do. I did not want to spend all of my life at this one particular place; I wanted to go beyond the place where I was. Father's death was the motivator for me reaching out for better things. I still worked two jobs; both were in the security field. The second job was working for the Portland School's special investigation department. I would pull stake-out duties with retired Sheriff's deputies, and former police officers. We would work in certain schools after dark to catch burglars steeling school equipment. Some of the things that were stolen were type writers, and other office equipment. We had some luck in catching some of the thieves. Some were caught on the streets trying to sell off the merchandise. There were others caught in other crimes and police connected them with certain burglaries. This job was also interesting. Other times I would serve as a school security officer, patrolling the school grounds, trying to keep the un- wanted visitors off the school grounds and keep the students of Washington high school on the school grounds.

My exposure to illegal drugs was the first time that I had ever seen or had knowledge of certain drugs. I often wondered why there were so many visitations by other young people from other schools or being out of school. They would either come to purchase drugs or sell drugs to the students. The school district made a strict law for people coming on the school grounds without having an excuse for being there. The students began to cut classes and leave the school grounds to meet their drug supplier. They would use their lunch break to leave the grounds so they could make contact with these drug suppliers.

Writing reports on what I had observed; when students left the school grounds or other students came on to the school grounds, a report had to be written. Some times police were called and an arrest were made. In my report, I explained exactly what I had observed, description of the people involved and the direction in which they departed. There were houses of prostitution near the school grounds and there were many arrests. One thing about these die hard drug suppliers, they knew the students had a demand for these drugs and they were going to find a way to supply it to them. One taken out of action and another would take their place. The most common drugs that were confiscated were marijuana, little red bennies. I am sure there were more types of drugs, but these were the most common. The school did not want the general public to know what was really taking place, they didn't want them to know this kind of thing were taking place under their noses. I worked for the school district for about three years. Then I left there to try my hand with the Oregon State Police; I studied hard to pass the State Police written examination and passed it with credibility. If accepted I would be the third Black to ever come on the State Police. The first was big Art Easter; the second Black to become a member was James Gray, a product of Jackson Mississippi. I was the third Black to ever become a member of the State Police. I had prayed to God about me joining the State Police. I had a dream of coming on to the State Police and in the dream, I was shown that I would receive the job, but I would not like it. God knew I would not like it, but he gave me my heart's desire and let me find out for my self that this was not the right thing for me to do. I thank God for showing me things that I would not like about the department that I could not see in the beginning. I knew God answered my prayer, I also knew he open my eyes to the truth about being too hasty in doing anything before hearing from him. I was to add to history, being the third Black to ever become a member of the State Police. Mother had prayed to God to show me a sign that I would not like what I was getting into. God listens to mother when she prays to him for things. I believe he answered her prayer. Again this was the power of prayer. She knew I would face racism and other factors that I would not like. I trained for six months and was training on the road with a training coach. He was a fair coach, he told me of the high points and the low points of patrolling. I wanted to show him my complete appreciation for helping me, but I could not find a way to be overly-happy in becoming a member.

Leaving the State Police; my mind had been made up, I told mother and wife of my intention to leave the State Police, and I gave them the reason why I would leave. The members of the department treated me as good as could be expected under the circumstances. There were few Blacks in the whole State of Oregon and there are people on the State that is from all over the State of Oregon, who still have some of those old ways of thinking about Blacks in any kind of a position. These people have had very little exposure to Blacks; they only know about blacks what they had been told by others. Most of these people live in the rural areas of Oregon. I left the department and was hired at the public transportation district of the tri-counties area. Now call; Tri-met. I started there as a bus driver, I knew nothing about a big bus or any other vehicle of this size. They trained me and I became confident that I could handle any thing that they put before me. In the beginning, the huge bus freaked me out, but as time went on my confidence grew. After six weeks of training, they put all that had made the grade on the Extra- Board. This is where a person would have a different route each day. Many of us made mistakes, some even got lost in trying to find their way along the route. This was one way of learning the tri-county area; you would learn the three county areas fast. I stayed on the extra- board for many years, the pay was good and you could work as many hours as you choose. They would have a sign-up every two or three months and you would have a chance to pick a regular route, this way a driver would know what he or she would be driving each day. You would also know what time you would get off work. This way they could make plans with their families.

Operating a bus for ten years, I learned much about the transportation system. I became a very good bus operator and by working the extra board, I learned all of the bus routes. When an operator could not come to work, an extra board operator had to take their place, you had to know the route and read the map for bus routes. The district had begun to hire more bus operators because the district was growing. They were expanding the system even farther out. They extended across the Columbia River into the State of Washington into Clark County, which the city of Vancouver and Hazel dell were served. The system is growing still to this day. Job at the transit system changed, I had passed a test for extra bus training instructor. My job was to join a host of other instructors in training all the new people that had been hired. My knowledge of the system, fares and bus riding rules eventually, qualified me for a fare inspectors position. I took the test for a fare inspector's position and was hired on a use as needed basis. We would eventually, have all of the new people trained and would have return back to our operation of the buses. I went back to my bus driving job and operated the bus about fifty percent of the time. The other times I was call off my route to fare inspection. There were many extra fare inspectors who were called by seniority when needed to fill shifts or to add a new team of inspectors. I worked as a part time fare-inspector for five to six years. One day I was called into the Chief inspector's office and ask me if I was ready to come into the department on a full- time basic?, The answer was yes, I had been waiting for a full time position for a long time. I knew the job well and had much knowledge of dealing with fare violations and passengers that were troublesome. When a passenger had been in the district's fare violations policy repeatedly, then we would issue those people a thirty, sixty or a ninety day suspension from riding the system or being on the district's property. There were laws in place to assure the riding public of a safe trip and as comfortable as possible. The system grew and so did crime and violations of the district's rules. Police was contracted out from various agencies in the tri-county area. They would sometime ride the buses with a fare inspector, we would ask for proof of their fares and the police made sure that they produced it. Many times people were arrested on other charges, warrants and other misconducts. The system had to be cleaned up if we were to go forward with the expansion of the rail system that was going to take place in the metropolitan area. Security was of the up-most importance.

Light rail system had been built, and everyone was happy, we could move people much faster and carry many more people on a single trip.

On a two car hook-he up, the rail car could carry nearly four hundred passengers. Rail proved to be such a success they had to expand the system into the three counties. Rail and buses combined to get people nearly anywhere they wanted to get to in the metropolitan area. Many people that lived in the state of Washington worked in the State of Oregon, mostly in the Portland area. The rail is now being built to serve the Vancouver, Washington area. Bridge for light rail across the Columbia River had to be built to connect the various bus routes that serve the Washington area. There's no doubt, the light rail system to serve the masses of people was the way to go. New buses were added to the system to up grade the aging fleet of buses. The system became the envy of other States and transportation districts through out the country. People from Europe were the engineers and the builders of the system. They were good in building light rail systems through out Europe. Bus routes continue to increase and rider ship were at an all time high. I knew this was where I wanted to spend the rest of my working life at. I had a good job and good benefits. The retirement was good and the job was stable for future years. I only needed this one job to fully support my growing family. Wife did not need to work for her to afford most things that she and the children wanted. My two oldest daughters were in high school and it would take a little more money to afford the things they needed as young women. Our families were growing up fast, sister and her family had to face the same problems as her family grew also. The oldest boys and the one daughter needed things to compete in high school. Samuel's two boys were not yet in high school, but he had already planned for that day, his wife was still working for the air lines. The big Surprise, Eli, our beloved brother that had passed away years ago, had left us with a new member of our family. Eli had fathered a son before he passed on. It took a long time for us to learn about this young man, he was about the same age of my son Michael, and close to the same age of my sister's third oldest son, three boys would become the best of friends and first cousins.

Mother was excited to have another grand son. If only we had known of him earlier, father would have met him. Eddie was his given name and he looked like his father Eli. He also had features of the Bryant's and he grew and studied history.

Eddie wanted to know more about his father, he was very young when Eli, his father passed away and did not know anything about him. His mother told him what she knew of him but he wanted to know more about him from his family. He talked to mother and asked questions about him, he wanted to know about him a little more. He wanted to know how he passed away, how long he had been sick, and what was his life like when he was living. We told him that" he was one of the kindest person that he would ever meet, he was loving and caring for people and animals, he loved nature and the out doors, he was a brave person and was not afraid of anything, we told him about our child hood and the things that happen to us growing up" mischief that we were involved in, most all these mischief were all in boys growing up in a exciting surroundings. Eddie was pleased to hear these things said about the man he never knew. We all wanted him to know about his grandfather also. We told him many stories concerning his grandfather. Told him how he had grown up on the farm, and some of the obstacles that he had to over come, how God had blessed him and his family to leave Mississippi and settle in Portland. He wanted to know more about his family history. He truly was pleased to be part of his father's family. Michael, my son and Jarrell my sister's third oldest son all were close to the same age and were the best of friends. They too liked the out doors. They liked to camp out and fish. Hunting was not their top priority in the out doors. They loved nature and the beautiful scenery, all of the wild life that would be all about. Father would have been pleased to see another grand son and the three being close to each other. Eddie's mother would come over to visit mother and the rest of the family when she could. We wanted her to feel at home with us and that she was part of the family, she was a decent lady and wanted her to feel if though she could talk to us about thing.

Mother growing older and needed more attention, now more than ever. She had lived in this house that God had shown in her dream many years before she received it. She had lived alone in this big house and never had any one to live with her after all the children had move out, and father had passed away. She would not live any where else but in this home that God had given her. We all made it a point to stay in contact with her on a daily basis, come over to her house on each Sunday and have our usual Bible study, praise and thanks meetings. We would have Bible study twice a month and visitation the rest of the time that we came over to her house. Mother was glad to have all of her children at her house all at the same time. We would sing songs and talked about her and father's marriage, and how they met at a church dinner. There were many memories of her early years, the strict rules of their parents that they had to obey. She talked about her younger brother that left the farm and went to Chicago as a young man to work there and make money to send back home to her parents. He took sick and had to be sent back to the farm where he had been born. He had taken low sickness and kept a high fever, he remained in bed until his death. Mother believed his sickness was a severe case of pneumonia; the family never left his side. They prayed and prayed for him to recover. But it did not seem to be in the plans for him to recover. Grandmother had told the rest of the family that she would pray for God to save his soul when his recovery did not seem to be in the plans of God. Uncle Samuel died at home in the bed with the family watching his last breath. This was only one of many stories that mother told to the children and grand children. She would always say if it was God's will for things to happen then it will happen and there is nothing, we can do to stop his will that would be done. We all learned much about her youth.

Chapter Six

Wife losing her father; Mae, my beloved wife had lost her father, he had been sick for a couple of months before he passed away. Mae took it very hard. She was the pick of the family; her father loved her very much and was given many special privileges. There were no doubts that she was one of his picks as favorite child. When I asked her hand in marriage, I had made him a promise that I would treat her as my wife and would do what was necessary to make her happy. He believed what I had told him and he hope us in any way that he could to make a success of our marriage. Carl was his first name, but I always called him" Mister Matthew", I always tried to treat him with the up-most respect and he respected me also. Mae and rest of her family had lost a good man. He was a good husband and a good father to his children. After my father had passed I looked up to him for the hard things of life, he always gave me good advice. Some things another man would be able to help you with, instead of a mother or another woman." Mister Matthew" would surely be missed. His oldest son took it badly; he did not recover from his lost for a long time to come. His wife, Wonder Matthew, had younger children that she had to provide for. This truly was a big lost for her. Money had to come in from other sources to help meet ends for house hold expensive. Everyone hope out the best way that they could. Her oldest daughter and her husband hope out when possible. We were a family and we all had a responsibility in making sure all were taken care off. Her oldest brother, Cornell, use to go fishing with me to try to escape some of the hurt that he had received from his father's passing. He enjoyed the privacy, quietness of being on the fish banks. Out doors is truly one way of, relieving stress by meditating. He always seems to be altogether in his thought process when he was fishing. He had even more fun when he caught a huge fish. His face lights up and he would become more talkative and energized. There were many things on his mind, he had lost his father and old memories had begun to come in. This is one thing that each person has to cope with in his own way; there is no magical way of dealing with situations such as this. We try to ease the thought process by finding other things to do and think about. I had to try to cope with my father's death. This is not an easy thing to do, someone you have known all of your life, and now they are not here any more. The ones that are left behind are the ones that suffer. The deceased have no knowledge of this world and the things they left behind, but we that are left alive will suffer many deaths. We have a hard time of letting go of the ones we love. Every human and animal faces this problem, releasing the ones that are dear to our hearts. Sometimes it seems if though you cannot go forward without the one that you love.

We are supposed to celebrate when one of our love one passes on to the other life, but it is natural for us that is left behind to do just the opposite, it is hard to come to the point where you are actually, glad and celebrate their passing into the unknown. We are told where we go when we passes on from this world to another. We are told that we have one of two places that we will go, depending on how you lived and God's forgiving us for our sins. If we have done what is asked of us by the Holy Scriptures then our destination is sealed, we would be with God in heaven forever. If we choose not to obey the Holy Scriptures, then there is another place that the un-believers and the disobedient will go forever, this place is call 'hell". Believe it, or not to believe it, this is what the Holy Scriptures teaches us. He also said that it is" not his will that any man should perish or go to hell". We choose where we want to spend our eternity at. God gave us all a free will to choose what direction we wanted to take. He could have created us as robots if he had wanted to, but he wanted to give us a free will to choose life and live, or to choose the way of sin and be condemned, which ever you choose it will be your eternity. This should not be such a hard decision to make, especially, knowing the consequences of the choices you have before you. We as human beings have an edge over the evil things of this world and Satan. When created us as human beings, he instilled a certain amount of goodness in every human that he had created. We have a certain amount of knowledge in right and wrong. People that have no knowledge of God or never heard his Holy name mentioned before, know a certain amount of right that god gave us. We have to learn about him to go beyond that amount of right that we have. This is why God have teachers and preachers to show us the way to go. Study his Holy word and learn about his kindness and his damnation. He did not force anything upon any of us; he gave us a direction in life which way we choose to follow. Cornell liked to talk about the mysterious things of life, the unknown, the earth's creation and all the animals and plants that have been created for life to be sustained here on Earth. This place was created specifically, for our habitation. I don't know whether God had intended for man to venture out of his earthly habitation. This is something that we probably will never really know. Some times things are allowed, he let man chase his dreams, although there might be lessons learned from never knowing when to quit, and to enjoy things on earth that he has placed here for our enjoyment. He wanted us to become good stewards over the things that he had placed here for our consumption. Greed is the one thing that separates us from the will of God. We as humans want more and more. We leave others of our species in poverty, and struggling to survive. I don't believe this was God's plan, to have his creatures to beg and be sad at the life that he has given us. Greed is the cause of eighty-five percent of the problems that we have in the world today. We had many discussions on why are there so many poor people in the world. This world took a turn from the time that God kicked the" Lucifer out of Heaven," the devil put his spirit down on earth to deceive man kind and wanting to compete with God." Lucifer's spirit has been here on earth every since"". Read the creation of the earth, starting in the first book of the Bible. "Lucifer was the most beautiful angel in heaven. He got beside him self and wanted to become God, he wanted to rule the Heavens and the entire universe". He lost his place in heaven when he became greedy, he wanted it all, this is the same attitudes we see here on earth today, not sharing the bounties of the earth, but to take it all for their own selfish reasons. This is why we have too much poverty and sickness in our world today. A few powerful people want it all. They wants control over everything, some would go to war to take what they want from other nations. If they can't buy it or steal it, then they would make war and take it from the weaker nations or individuals. This fishing trip was a success; it had Cornell, thinking of what it really was all about. We went fishing many times after and caught much fish. I could never get him to go hunting. I believed he would have liked to sit around the camp fire and exchange information with others in the hunting party. Mae, my wife and his sister, liked to see him and I having so much in common, she knew this would occupy his mind in doing something that he was interesting in. My family as a whole were doing well, most over came the lost of their grandfather. However, this was the second time that they were faced with the loss of both, grandfathers. Children accepted it better than the adults.

Jack, my friend and the first friend that I made when I came to Portland, joined the Guards with me and he would go to monthly drills and to summer camp with me. I was glad to have him aboard; we were in the same company and in the same platoon. He eventually, persuaded his first cousin to join also. His name was Billy Bridges, and he had gone to the technical school with us. We had much fun together and worked together in our youth, picking strawberries, beans, washing cars and mowing lawns. We had done much together and were good friends. Military strict rules and regulations were not for Jack or Billy. Jack had begun to miss drills and sometime was late in arriving to the meetings. The authorities got tired of Jack missing drills and inducted him into the regular army for three years. I was sorry to see jack leaving to go to Fort Polk, Louisiana, this was a new experience for him and his family, and he had a wife now and had to be away from her for a three year period. He would only come home on military leave and very special occasion. . Jack had really gotten him self in trouble this time with the Government. He had a hard time of adjusting to the army's way of life. I received letters from him while he was going through his basic training. He told me about the swamps, the snakes, alligators and other insects, hot and humid weather in the swamps. They were preparing him for the terrain in Vietnam. If he went over there, this is the type of terrain that he would have to face. After training, Jack came home for two weeks. We had much fun and he had much to tell about Louisiana the weather, the people and the swamps. He would go to a fort in Alabama. He would remain there for a while, until they figure out what his next move would be. He enjoyed his stay at home and his wife was glad to see him. He did not want to go back, but he did not want to make a second mistake with the Government. Jack was learning not to fool around with the army. Jack had been in the army for more than six months, he had finished his basic training, now he was going to school for what he had qualified for on military testing scores. He had scored high in the missile defense program; it was a good job to train in. He completed his training there and went to Missouri to finish his obligation to the army. Jack did very well in missile defense he could not adjust to the strict discipline of the military all the orders that were given and had to be obeyed. He could soldier when he wanted to do so. The orders that were given, he didn't like. Billy was drafted into the army and was sent to Fort Ord, California to take his basic training. After seeing what had happened to his first cousin, he knew he had to shape up or the army would make it hard for him. They would extend his time in the army if he did not measure up to expectations. Some people can cope with military life and there are others who cannot. Billy finished his basic training and received a two week leave. He had earned this vacation time after finishing his basic training. He was glad to come home to see family and friends. Billy looked good in his summer brown khakis uniform. He looked like a real solider and he acted like a real soldier. He was more disciplined and more attentive than verbal. The army always breaks a man's spirit first and they will break your body, preparing the individual for the rigors of war. Your body will be in good physical condition when you finish your basic training. Billy and friends sat around and talked about the old times that we had, the parties, the girls and other things we had done when we were in our school days. Now I am married, and most of the old friends have families of their own and we had to face our responsibilities. We all had dreams of what we had hoped to accomplish in the future for our families. Billy, enjoyed his two weeks vacation at home and went to another military post, there he would go to school and train in the job that he had scored the highest on. Billy would remain on this post until he finishes his on the job training. Both, first cousins were in the army on different posts and never got to see one another when they came home on a two week leave. Jack had nearly finished his three years in the army and would be coming home for good. His family would be very proud of him staying with the army and finishing up his obligation. He can now feel proud that he had accomplished this task.

Jack, had a lot to catch up on at home, he had to get his family on the right road to success. He said he had been putting money aside to purchase a home for his family, and he would be looking for a decent home not too far from his parents. Jack had three younger sisters and one older brother, the brother who had served four years in the United State air force. Mostly of his time were served over seas in Germany. Jack's parents were very nice people; they always treated me with respect. They wanted to know how my family was doing, all the children and wife's family were doing. The Johnson's were good people. Jack had come from a good family. I don't know why he had trouble obeying orders in the Guards. He said that he adapted to the military when he was drafted into the U.S. army. Now that he is home, he is ready for his responsibilities. Some people can adapt to mostly any situation, and there are others who just don't fit in to situations so easy, they have to work to adjust. It was an adjustment that he had to make in order to full- fill his military obligation. One thing he had to do was to obey orders and carry out the mission that has been given to you. Regardless of how you feel about taking orders and military conduct, they all specialize in breaking your spirit and your body down. When they release you from service, you would be a better person coming out than what you were going into the military services. I learned much in the military. It gave me more confidence to handle the ups and downs of life, and so did it give Jack more confidence. We both, would walk the journey of life in our own way at our own pace, we have the same destination in mind, to raise our families, and for them to be happy and prosper, and to walk this life's journey knowing we had reached the goals in life that we had set for ourselves and our families.

Family occurred. This time was her mother that passed away. The family had to weep, and become sorrow once more. Her mother was loved by all, people that knew her were saddened by her passing, her children took it very hard, and she was the rock of her family, we all depended on her "wise advice on many issues". She loved all that had known her. Her parents had been married for many years and when her husband passed away, she seems to have lost the will to continue to live without him. The children had no one to look after them now. She kept them on the right road to success. She kept the family together and taught them the way to travel this life's journey. No one can tell you how you should take this tragedy; each family member has to find his or her own way of dealing with it. I have had many deaths in my family, each time it happens seems like it was the first. You can never adjust to death of a love one. Wonder had left nine children behind, five boys and four girls, and many grandchildren. They all had to come together and remain a family. This is what their parents would have wanted, the family staying together and helping one another. The oldest of the family took up the leader ship role of their mother. She had a family of her own and would divide her time between two families. Her husband and two daughters and her younger brothers and a younger sister, Cornell her oldest brother had the role of disciplinarian; he would keep the four boys in a straight line. He took the role as father or guardian to the boys. The baby girl had her overseers also; there were three other women in the family to keep her in line with family values. This is the way a family is supposed to do, take up the responsibilities of their parents when they are no longer with them. Many family members in a situation such as this have a tendency of going astray and no one to keep them on the right pass to become a success in life. Then they would start their lives already in a down fall. People from all around us use to take a hand in trying to help raise children that were without their parents. Any adult had the God given authority to help raise children in the correct way. It truly takes a whole village to raise one child. This is the best way to have a successful community. We all are our brother's keeper, whether we want to be or not. These rules were set up my God, and this is the correct way for humans to live. Each generation carries the baton to assure the race in life is positively won.

Arthur's baby brother came out of Jackson, Mississippi to seek a new way of life; he had finished high school and wanted to come out to Portland where his other three brothers were. He found a job at the same plant that we all had worked at when we migrated to Oregon. Here he made a successful life for himself. Benny, work at this plant to this day, he is nearly at the retirement age. This is the only job he worked on since coming to Portland. A few years later, he had his baby sister to come out of Mississippi and into Portland to start a new life; she worked and also became successful in her life. The whole lesson learned from this was, family members helping one another, when one would become situated in the surroundings, they would give a helping hand to pull other members of the family up from poverty and injustices. We were from the State of Mississippi, and we all knew how things were in that State for Black people. There are some that will never leave the State, regardless of what they were going through. There are many reasons for not leaving State I suppose, but they did not want to leave the place where they were born, where their ancestors were born and lived all of their hard lives. Much history, old memories and education are the primary reasons for some not wanting to leave the State. Many farmers and share- croppers had nothing else to look forward to in life, but staying put where they were. Although things could be much better there, they knew what they were up against staying put where they were. However, if they left the farm, they would not be sure of how life for them would turn out to be. We might be out in the far west, but our thoughts and our roots grow deep in the same State they are in. Persuasions and motivations were the only thing that moved our parents out west to Portland and other western towns and cities. Washington, Oregon, California seems to be where we set our roots in.

Opportunity was the single thing that the family seek, a good paying job, a decent place to live, and good education for their children. From these points in life they would be able to make a much better life for their families. As our children become adults and began to raise their own families in the near future, our greatest desire is for them to become educated and equipped with the right tools to face an ever more educated society. We hope they all will finish their schooling and be well prepared to face the world as it is. We as Black people, really don't have a choice in education, we know we don't want to go back where we have just come from in life. The alternative is to keep pressing forward, with a good education and never forget God, never turn your back on the one who had blessed us to be where we are and where we want to be. The world is no more just white against black and black against white. The whole world is getting smaller, through communication, transportation and a global economic economy. Competition is on the rise with students of all nationalities competing for the same jobs as American students. Without a well rounded education we would be left behind and back where we had just left from. I hope that all students will take the advantage of the opportunities that is before them. This journey through life is a long journey. The good thing about our journey is that we all had trail blazers that paved the way for us to have an easier trip during our travel. We as Black people have endured more than any other group or race of people in the struggle for freedom, equal rights, education, employment, areas to live in, hospitalization, job promotions and many more things that would advance a particular people. This is why education is not an option for us if we want to continue our journey from poverty to success. I have seen many things in life's journey that have kept us at the bottom of the economic ladder. Much have to do with us not taking advantage of the opportunity when it is made available to us. The other part of it is the institutional racism that exists. We all are working toward trying to close the gap on this kind of discrimination practices. This is a joint effort, we, the government, and cooperation. People also need a renewing of their minds, old ideas and old customs, classification of humans that is called inferior or wanting to be superior to one another. The world is changing; we need to jump aboard if we want to see a more positive world in our life time. We should work for a better tomorrow for the future generations. Computers, transportation, communication, all have made the world smaller and more knowledgeable of other people and other cultures of the world. We all should do our part in making it a reality. It is true, that no man or no country is an island unto it's self. We are in a survival mode together. No longer can one country say that they don't need any other country to survive in this world.

Faith and Christianity; in my study of Christianity, the definition is suppose to be Christ like. Any person any where in the world can easily see that we have missed the mark as to what Christ was all about." How can we as a nation say that we are Christ like people? When we have knowingly, done nearly the opposite of what Christ was and still is all about". This is a challenge to us all to see exactly, where we measure up to in being like Christ. How can we say that we love "Christ" whom we have never seen him and hate one another that we see each day? we go out of our way to make other people of the world lives miserable. Why were there laws made to keep people in a certain classification and to keep them from participation in the world of plenty for everyone? The reality is it should not be any starving nations of the world. This earth was created to support all of it inhabitants. If we were good stewards and shared with each other, and it was not for the greedy consumers, there would be enough food and other materials to supply the whole world. There are many that made their fortunes by working hard and putting their talents to work, but there are many who rob, steal, cheat, deceive and any other way they can get to the top of the economic ladder, leaving the hardworking, honest people struggling at the bottom of the pole. Why people refuse to face up to the problem that confronts our world? We never hear the truth about the real problem. It seems to be much easier not to mention the true facts about this terrible atrocity to man kind. Why does one person or one family have so much and another struggles to put food on his table? Most of the inequities come through greedy people who consume more than they should or need to survive. I know there will always be some people that will excel, there will be some that will never do it for one reason or another, but even at that it should not be all the wealth in the hands of one or two percent of the worlds population, they controls ninety-five percent of the world's wealth and power. Our world's system condones the corruption, the greed, deceit, robbery, murder, lies, wars and many other things that contribute to the world that we have inherited. It all started centuries ago, the trend had been set for future generations; this is the world that they left the future generations to live in.

A new day is near by. As the world become better educated to what the true problems are, and who and what is causing it, began to unite the nations of the world to fight against such injustices and poverty. I know these things will play out in God's own time. The spirit of" Lucifer" inhabited this planet many thousands of years ago and his deceitful, murderous tactics exist today. He, God will let man run his course on earth and then he will come back to set up a perfect government on earth. Biblically, the Bible has to be full filled. It is our duty to work hard in trying to correct the wrong things that we have done to this planet and its inhabitants. It is the younger generation that will govern the type of world they want to live in. Many of the older generations have failed to give us a better world to live in. Those who had the power to make it a better world, refused to try to change the power structure in the world we now inherited. Progress can be seen, it may not be as fast as we want it to, but some progress in some things are very visible. The spiritual improvement will only come from God, that's when man's heart will be changed, in his own time. This is truly the real concrete way that man will ever change in deeds and in his thoughts. I see many races of people coming together in trying to form a more perfect world to live. This is something that were very rare, to see so many races and nationalities coming to this country to learn about our culture and its people. Communication, transportation has brought us to another level in how we think of our world's neighbors. We cannot any longer tell other nations of the world what to do and when we should do it. There are more nations that are having more influence on the world's stage. Living in the south and reading about things that were happening all around me, I began to feel like we were fenced in and could not escape. It took father many years to answer the call of freedom. This was a whole new way of life for us. Making a decent wage and purchasing the home that you could have and a family having a chance to succeed in life. Although we have a long way to go, yet we have traveled a long journey and made much progress along the way. An opportunity through education is the key to reality.

The march to freedom did not come easily, there were many people participating in the freedom marches, people of all races and religious persuasions marched in support of freedom and justice. There were many who lost their lives, which were beaten and jailed for this cause. This is the reason why we as Black people should take advantage of every opportunity that is before us. Nothing good ever happens without a fight for it. We now enjoy the things that our ancestors only dreamed off. We are seeing the reality of it all. The movement was and still is a joint operation between all of honest, God fearing people around the Globe. Many knew the way we were going could not be sustained indefinitely. This was a marathon race with a relay team in the mix. Each generation picks up the baton and continues the race until it is won. Young Blacks should not become complacent in this race. We have not won the race yet, regardless of the advancements that have been made. We should continue to reach for the stars. Young people need to know more about their past, so they could have a deeper appreciation of where they are going. Some time people have to know where they came from in order to determine a future.

My children have grown up and most of them have finished high school. There is one left to finish school, my baby girl, Carla Lynn. Another year for her in school and she would be graduating and on to college. Michelle, the oldest child is going to school and working part time with the Army corps. Of Engineers, Joyce is working for the Blue Cross Blue Shield insurance firm. Michael, the only son is working at the Portland International air port. He has plans of attending a technical college. We hope that all of them will do well in life. When Carla finishes high school, her intention is to go to medical school.

Our parents are happy to see their grandchildren finish high school. Father would have been extremely proud of his grandchildren. However, he only went to the third grade in school and part-time at that. Mother, she managed to finish the eight grades and she had a good I.Q., and was appointed to teach the rest of the students in her class. I often wonder how far she would have gone in school if she would have had the opportunity to do so. After the eighth grade, she would have to go to one of the larger cities to receive a higher education. She remained sharp with numbers and her studies with current events that were taking place. It was her that hope me purchase my home that I am living in. She wanted to see all of us purchase a place that we could call home for our families. As a mother, she had done everything that her and father had spoken about before he passed away. She had lived the life that God had expected of her. Sister and her family were doing well. Her three oldest children had finished high school and were attending college and working. Samuel, the youngest of the children, was married and had two boys that were doing well also. His youngest son had an exceptional high I. Q.; he wanted to join the U. S. air force. He received recommendations from the following public officials; principle at the technical school that he graduated from, Oregon State senator, Governor, mayor, and concerned citizens. All of these individuals had to approve his request before he could enter the academy. All parties signed for him to attend the school. His schooling would be for a fighter pilot. During his schooling, he would continue to make high marks at the academy. When he graduated and was shipped out to other countries on other U.S. bases, he begins to gain rank at a very quick pace. He went from Lieutenant to Captain, to Major and then to Lieutenant Colonel. He achieves all of this in very short order. He now teaches Flight Engineering to the fighter pilots. He is a young man and if he chooses, he would be able to retire in a few more years. He still would be a young man when he retires, if he chooses to do so, his oldest son have an entertainment business, recruiting young new talent for his musical entertainment business. Only the youngest boy has married, he met his wife in the service. She is from South Africa, and was here going to school to become a chemist. They have traveled all over the world and spent time with her parents in South Africa. Her parents and siblings all educated.

There are many young people from all over the world, coming to America for their education. Many Americans students are in school and doing well, but it seems if though the media concentrates on the negative the silent majority who is doing well in school and beyond. Wife's nephew, Damon made it to the professional basketball ranks, and done well for himself. He started out for a love for basketball from the time the basketball was larger than him. He could barely hold the ball when he was a very young boy. He was not giving up on his dreams of becoming a professional ball player. He trained day and night to achieve what he wanted in life. This paid off for him; he broke or tied every major basketball record in grade school, high school, and in college. He was drafted as the number two spot on the draft date for the NBA. He went on to become the Rookie of the year in the NBA. He had a dream and he continued to chase it. Damon has been in the NBA. For fourteen years. He was well liked and well known in the State of Oregon, the city of Portland and the State of Arizona, where he attended college. More of us should become involved in teaching our young people how to avoid trouble and stay in school. We should work as mentors to those students who came from a family less fortunate than ours. For one reason or another, our students do not show an interest in what the schools have to offer. Some feel like what's the use of trying to achieve a higher learning, things just will be the same as usual. They should be taught that it is pertinent to learn as much as they can learn and to reach for the stars. They have to be prepared to meet the challenges that are ahead of them. Things have changed, and are changing every day. Avoid those students who refuse to want less in life, if they reject the truth about their future then there isn't too much more that you can say to them. Don't let them pull you down or hold you back from achieving your higher goals. Losing these types of people may be the best thing for you. It has to be one way or the other. Either you will lose your sights on your future, or you will lift him up from his road to no where. A real friend tries to elevate their friends to a higher and better way of living and playing.

I worked for the school as a mentor; some of these students were behind in most of their classes. They only came to school because they had to do it. Not because they were seeking a higher learning, they wanted to put their time in at school and then hit the streets with their buddies. Some were involved in drugs, prostitution, robbery, burglary and other criminal acts. When arrested for these deeds, they were automatically put into the criminal system. They then had one strike against them, in trying to find a decent paying job to support a good life style. Being rejected on many occasions, frustration sets up and they begin a life of a career criminal. Serious injuries or even death occurs in these situations. This is why it is so important that we start out with these troubled students, as soon as we locate the problem that confronts the un-motivated students. The earlier we spot the wayward students the better it will be to get them turned around in their life style. It took me a while to understand exactly what was going on, right under the school's jurisdiction, drugs were being brought on to and sold right on the school's play ground, the hall ways, cafeteria, and any other place a student could sell or purchase drugs. I know the schools have an obligation to the community, but they hid much of the things that were taking place under their control. They did not want to arouse the community concerning the situation at their schools. I would not speak of these things happening at schools if I did not have a first hand knowledge of it happening. I was there, I wrote many reports on the situation, some students were disciplined and others received a slap on the back. However, the problem grew worse; the police had to set up dragnets to apprehend the pushers and the drug users, the prostitutes and other criminals that used the schools as a drug haven. Many of these suspects were in their early to late twenties; some were students that attended the same school. We all have a hand in trying to make the communities a better place to live for all of our families and neighbors. Being observers and report un-usual things to the school or the police. If we work together, we could clean up our communities and the criminals would have to leave. The students would become more motivated to learn when they were in school. They would see what the consequences of quick, fast money would lead them to if caught, either jail or death. They should be taught what the end's result will be if they continued to follow this particular life style. It is sweet, they think. And it is very short. If it is stressed up on them all of the negative application of this type of life styles this offers, then I believe students would re-consider their lives before it would be too late for them to make a change.

My belief, drugs, and other criminal acts is put or brought into our communities to intentionally keep our communities from achieving the things that we pursue in life. There is an element of corrupt people that want to see the communities fail. Their job is to make sure that these communities do not succeed in up-ward mobility. I don't know who they are, but I do know that they exist. These people have no conscious. As long as they could make money off the ignorant and under privilege people of our communities, they wouldn't care who they sold the poison to. Unfortunately, our young and weakest of our communities suffer the most. They think that the approach to this way of life is where it's all about. Soon they become hooked, and then they would do any thing to have the drugs. This is what the provider wants; he needs a steady user of his merchandise so he can remain in business. He or she doesn't care who they sells it to as long as they sells and make a profit from doing so. If you are hooked on using it and cannot afford to pay right then for the merchandise, they will give you credit. Now you are really involved. You owe the seller, you cannot pay the bill that you owe, and you become desperate for drugs and to pay the seller. You have a choice to steal, to rob or burglarize some home to sell merchandise to pay your debt and to receive more drugs. If the seller receives either one, something horrible usually, occurs, bad injuries to you or death, unless the police intervene first. Either way, you are a loser, Jail or death.

Chapter Seven

We all make choices in life, the consequences of each is laid out before us, if we make the wrong choice and suffers the consequence of having made that choice, we and we alone is responsible for the one we made. If we would have only listened to people that had talked to us concerning these issues, then we would not be caught up in these situations. The only exceptions, is a young person that did not receive any teaching from their parents or guardians, concerning what to watch out for while alone, away from their home. It is true, many children were born during the drug revolution and did not receive any training on staying away from drugs, and instead, they were encouraged to use drugs and alcohol. The young people should have special consideration in treatment and teaching of the right way to go. It is a shame to our society, when we encourage our young children to become drug and alcoholic dependencies, when parents teaches their children that it is ok to engage in such practices, they either don't care about the society that they are bringing their children up in, or what effect it have on their child growing up as a whole. They should want the very best things in life for their children, but this is not the way for them to achieve a success in life. Many of the parents brought these children into the world when they were addicted to drugs and or alcohol themselves, and had no time in trying to teach their children the right way of growing up, therefore, they have brought them up to become a burden to society. The things that the parents should do for the children, the taxpayers now have done for them. They forget that doing their own thing effects more than themselves. They throw their burden up on the tax payers. The fault is not the children's fault; it is the parents that brought them into this world. It is their responsibilities to care for, and teach them the correct way to go. During my employment at the transit district, I saw much concerning run-away, children without any place to lay their heads, they would ride on transit trains and buses until the system closed down, then they would go down town to stay. . This was a terrible thing to see, young people without a place to go. Many had no food for days. Some had left their home in far away places. They came from the south, the north, east and western part of the country. There were some that chose this type of life style. There were some who had no choice in doing what they did. Many parents kicked them out of their homes for one reason or disobedience is the primary cause of them being homeless. There is hope for these people, regardless of what they think. They can turn their lives around, if they really tried to do so. Help is out there waiting for them to make the first step toward reform. Many were put out of their homes because of some mistake that they made. They should not be penalized for life, because of the mistake or disobedience in their home.

These youths should be welcomed back home and talk about the problems that they may have. They are part of a whole that has gone astray. Having a true dialogue is the best way to accomplish this goal. Sitting down talking to each other, let each person explain his or her story the way they see it. Let them know that they are still loved and the family want them back into the family's fold. The family should welcome them with open arms. We all were teenagers once in our life and should to some extent, be sympathetic to what they are going through. They want to prove their man or woman hood and think they should be given more slack or liberty, to do things that may be against the family's rules and policies that are laid down for the family to abide by. More young men rebel against their parents than young women; they want to rule their own roost, forgetting that they are still in their parent's home. This alone doesn't mean that the student is a bad person. The student made the wrong choice of being a rebel. Many students go through the same problems at home, they forget to honor their parents and obey the rules of the home. Parents should tell the student where they stand on certain issues that are based upon the rules of the house. Don't wait until the rules are broken before telling the students of the consequences that will take place if they are broken. This way the student should have no doubt where he stands with the parents. Obedience is the most important of all these rules and house regulations. Parents have to be firm with their children. If they don't follow up with some kind of consequence for their disobedient, the children will not have respect in what you are telling them, they will become more disobedient and rebellious. No parents want to be too hard on their child, but they have to do what is necessary to gain compliance to their rules and regulations. This is God's law." Spare the rod and you will spoil the child". There was a reason for God to tell the parents not to spare the rod, keeping them in line with the right way of raising their children. Children will go as far as you allow them to go. The truth is, children to some extent, want to be loved and chastised when they get on the wrong track. If parents allow them to do or say anything that they choose to say or do, then many will think that their parents really don't care about them. Some parents refuse to be on the wrong side of their children by allowing them to do and say what they will. Exercising their responsibilities as parents is the correct way. You rule them or they will rule you.

I have traveled the journey from youth to man hood, from marriage with children and fatherhood to grandfather, and I have been there, seen what parents is up against and the rules that should be applied to raising their love ones. These family rules were carried out by my parents, and by my parent's parent. If you believe in the teaching of Biblical principles and faith in what the Bible tells us to do, then you should not be hesitant in carrying out these principles. All of the rules for raising a healthy family have been laid out before we were born to this earth. God knew from day one what we humans would face on earth. The rules and regulations were thought off before we occupied this planet. God knew that" Lucifer would put obstacles in our way to try to deter us from serving him" This was the mission of the evil one. Remember, he did not want to serve God any more; he wanted to become God, so God kicked him from Heaven and stripped him of his power in Heaven. He occupied the endless spaces in the universe where he could set up camp and deceive any and everything that he could. He wanted war against God and his Holy Angels. When we were created by God, the evil one made sure he would occupy and influence the creatures that God had placed on this planet, called earth. "Lucifer and his influence has been here with us ever since". In the last day to come," Lucifer will be locked up and eventually, destroyed with all of his works and his earthly supporters". This is God's promise to the inhabitants of this earthly planet, he allowed the evil one to mingle with the inhabitants here; God gave us a way out of yielding to the ways of" Lucifer and his many temptations." We alone cannot defeat the evil one, but with God's Holy teachings tells us how to resist these temptations and not yield to them. Prayer and resistant is the alternate.

Michelle, my oldest daughter falls in love. She met her future husband at the annual Rose Festival event. Ships from all over the free world come to Portland to participate in the annual Rose Festival activities. Some ships from Australia, Great Briton, Canada, U.S., and other vessels from other countries. All come to participate in the annual event, the crowd that they draw and the interest that the people bring to the festival. The ships that come in to the port, draws people from around the world and many cities in the U.S., and territories, this is truly a grand event. Michele's friend was introduced to the family. His name was Royal Forbes; he said he was from the Island of the" Grand Turks, called Caucus" his parent and some of his sisters and brothers are still in the Cayucos. He came to the U.S. on a sponsorship from an U.S. business cooperation and went to school in Boston, on a grant that was allocated through the same cooperation that sponsored him to come to the U.S., he worked as a carpenter and home builder for the company that was responsible for him being here in the States. He finished his schooling and joined the U.S. Navy. He had made a high mark in taking his placement test with the Navy. His job would to be to trouble shoot and repair the equipment aboard the ship that he served on all the boilers, refrigeration, heating, cooling and any other operation of small engines and cooling systems. He said he had traveled over the world with the navy and had seen much, met many different nationalities and races of people. He had learned much in his travel around the world. He said he was "fond of Michele, and if we approved, he would continue to write and call when possible to Michele." We all liked the young sailor, the way he carried himself as a young man and a sailor in the U.S. Navy. They should be proud to have a young man such as him. He was a highly intelligent and quick to learn young man. He wanted to know more about the American way of life. He also wanted to know why young Blacks don't take advantage of the opportunities that is before them. Here in the U.S. he saw unspeakable opportunities to take advantage off. On the Island where he came from, they had to struggle to survive. Fishing was the main food of support. Some private vegetable and fruit orchards are where they got most of their other food. He sees so much here in the U.S. that we all should be thankful off. Eat what we wanted, and as much as we wanted.

Marvin, the oldest nephew and my sister's oldest child, had been married for more than a year. This young lady that he married came from a highly educated family. Her mother was a school teacher and her father had a good paying job also. Her sisters and her brothers, either had graduated from college or was still going to college. Marvin and Jo Anna had known each other for many years. Even doing high school years they were friends. Jo Anna, still work for the same company as she did when she was in high school. Marvin worked at a computer factory, they to have done well for themselves. They are involved in the church. Marvin likes music and plays the guitar for his choir. They are very active in the church. Mother was very proud of Marvin and his wife, him being the first to get married of the grandchildren. One by one the grandchildren had begun to marry and start their own families. Sister had one down and four more to go, three more boys and one girl yet to marry. I had the oldest girl to marry off. One boy and two more girls that would eventually, marry off. Royal, the young sailor who had drawn fond of Michele had been talking marriage in the near future, and he wanted to know how we would feel about him becoming our son-in law. There weren't much we could say about it, they loved each other and this was the key to a happy marriage. We gave him our approval and they soon set a date to marry. Sister's next oldest boy, Anthony or [Tony] was going to school in California and had met his mate in Oakland, California. They were in college and had fallen in love with each other. He soon wrote home to his parents, informing them of his intention to get married. A date was set and they got married in Oakland, California. He remained in California and ran his own business, and promotes young talent, comedy and some acting promotions. His business is becoming more popular each year.

Cathay is the only girl in sister's family of five. She and Michele is close to the same age, they are close first cousins. They have always communicated with each other and talked about their personal problems. Cathay confers with Michele on her personal problems before making a decision. They were more like sisters than first cousins. She had been dating this young man for a few years, about the time Michele had been dating Royal, her future husband. They would get married a year apart from each other. Her future husband was given the name of Samuel, [Sam] he was a person that took the advantage of every opportunity to go to school and to achieve. They loved each other and were involved in church. They eventually, became husband and wife, Cathay, went to college and received a degree.

Michele and Royal were married. They had a beautiful wedding at the same church that we have attended since moving to Portland. Michele was well known among the members of the church. Many of the same members are still there. They remember when she was born; they also remember when my wife was pregnant with Michele. They remember when Mae, my wife fell when carrying Michele. Someone saw what had happened out side, coming onto the church's front lawn, the Pastor asked for her to stand and for prayer from the congregation, for her well being and her child which was Michele. Her birth was a success. She was a healthy baby. Everyone took a likeness to her ever since that day. The wife was not injured in any way. God had protected her and the child. Michele and Royal had a beautiful wedding and a big reception afterward. They received many well wishes and gifts from members, neighbors and friends. Everyone offered their help in getting them started in life. Mother was very pleased for them also. Royal mother came out west from the Grand Cayucos Island, this was the first time she had ventured this far into the U.S., and she was pleased and wished them well. They wanted her to live with them in an apartment house. She did not want to leave her native born land in the Grand Cayucos Island. There is where the rest of her family lives. Her husband passed away many years ago and her family had to stick together to survive. However, she has a son and a daughter living in Miami, Florida, and she visit them frequently. She like the U.S., but would not want to live here. The rest of her life will be in the Grand Cayucos.

Cathay was also married in the same church that they had grown up in. She was well known also. Her father was and still is involved with the choir, he is an elder of the church and he participates in many functions of the church. These marriages were happy times for the parents. They had given their stamps of approvals to their spouses. We hoped and prayed for their happiness and prosperity in this world of un-certainty. Royal first job in Portland was at the infamous Lloyd Center shopping mall. He had a job working as a facility engineer; this is what he was trained for in the U.S. Navy. He went to school and kept up-grading his skills. He worked there for a few years and received high marks for repair and installing boilers, refrigeration, air condition, heating and other electrical and mechanical hard ware. Royal kept up with the latest equipment in his field, as he learned and progressed, he reached for higher goals in his field of trade. There were openings in public works, in the county of Multnomah, Oregon. He applied for the job, passed the testing with a high score and was hired. He started as an apprentice and worked his way up the ladder to a journeyman engineer. He worked as a journeyman for years and then went to school to become a foreman. He is on this job this day. He never gave up on pursuing the job that he had been trained for. Michele had her first child. It was a girl and had features of her mother and her father. She was a beautiful baby and adored my both families. The new family purchases a home in a middle class neighborhood and was pleased. The family lives in the same house today. They only had the one child. She was given the name; Lauren "Whitney" Forbes. This was a beautiful name for a beautiful child. This was a happy occasion for every one. Mother has now seen her grandchildren and her great grand child. This made her proud to be a great grand mother. Wife's mother and family were also pleased to have a great grand daughter in the family. Father never had a chance to see his great grand daughters; he had passed on many years before. However, wife's father was able to see his great grand daughters, before he passed on. Cathay, sister's only daughter, was near bringing a new baby into the family. The time had come for her to go to the hospital and ever one was on pins and needles. They were wondering what it would be. Some wanted a girl, and there were some who wanted a boy. We all wanted it to be healthy and normal. When the time came, it would be a healthy handsome looking boy. This made all proud. His grand father was especially pleased to have another grand son. We loved him.

We all kept the tradition alive; twice a month we all would come over to mother's home to have Bible studies and to offer assurance to mother that we all still loved her. We would pray and sing hymns, and mother would play the piano. Afterwards, we would sit and chat about things, sometime about the past, and sometimes about the future. We all gave honor to father who was responsible for all of us to be here. Michele left the corps. of engineers and started a job with the transit system. She went into the customer's assistance department. This is the job she has been on to this day. She did not have to worry about a baby sitter; her mother was more than willing to baby sit for her. Besides, she had a way with babies; she had the right touch and patience to work with young children. She had raised four babies of her own and worked around many others. She had definitely had the right patience and the know how to baby sit. Mother would baby sit when the young mothers had special things to do, such as going to the doctor or the dental office. As time went by, sister's second oldest son, Anthony [Tony] had a young baby boy in Oakland, California. This is where he made his home when he was attending college there. He had married a California girl, and this is where her parents lived. They came home to Portland on some occasions. He introduced his wife to the rest of his family and she was well received as member of the family. One by one we were losing a member through marriage, but gaining another through marriage. Soon all of our children would get married and we would be in the same situation that we had left our parents in. It is hard to see all of your children leave home, but you knew soon or later that they would find some one that they wanted to spend the rest of their life with. Raise a family, see them grow and be successful in life. So life goes on, one leaf falls off and another take its place. We left our beloved home to start a family; our parents had the same feeling for us when we left home, as we do for our children. Few parents will ever say that they were glad when their children left the safety net of home.

Her friend had set a date to get married. Joyce introduced her future husband to the family. He said he wanted to marry her, he hope that we would approve of it. He gave the name of Michael Johnson, he had lived in Portland for many years, and he had gone to school here and came to Portland when he was five years old. His parents were from Houston, Texas. His father worked on a merchant ship and was traveling around the world most of the time. He comes home every three or four months. He said him and his sister were the only children in the family. His mother worked at a computer factory in the next county, which is a forty-five minute drive. His mother had approved of the marriage. A year had gone by and they became husband and wife. Another year went by and they added to their family. Another girl was born into the family. She as the others was a beautiful girl. She had features of her mother and of her father. She received the name of Rhea Mae. There would be one grander child added to my family. Two years after Rhea was born, Joyce had a second child, this was a girl also, and the name given to her was Reyanna, she was another beautiful baby that had many features of the Bryant's and her father, Michael Johnson. She was the last grand child in my family. She was admired by all of her relatives on both sides of her family. We would have six females and only one male in my family. I would have two son-in laws and one son. We were still out numbered by females in the family. Carla, my baby daughter never had any children. Michael my only son never got married and had no children. Over all, the amount of males in the family out numbered the females in the family. My sister had four boys and one girl. My baby brother had two boys and one female. My brother Eli, who had passed away many years before, left one son behind, and I had three girls and the only son. We did have our share of boys to carry the Bryant's name sake forward. We were proud of them all, male or female. We were a unified family and we operated as one family. When one member of the family was down and out, we gave as much support to them as possible. When one was sorrowful, then we all felt the pain. We wanted each other to be happy and to act happy.

Wonder passes on; Mae's mother passed away after a long illness. She had worked in the ship yards during the Second World War, cleaning departments on board ships that were being repaired or being built. After many years after she had left, she took sick with a lung disorder. She did not smoke nor did she drink alcohol. The doctors had diagnosed her of having asbestos on her lungs. It took a long time to find the cause of her infection, the asbestos had settled deep into her lungs that were hard to locate in a peculiar place. When they located the asbestos, they tried to scrape it off her lungs; the material had lodged into her lungs and was fine as refined power. They could not remove the asbestos, it had gone too far and there were nothing that the doctors could do to save her from this deadly disease. It was ruled that the asbestos from the ship yard was the cause of her death. The family took this death of their mother very hard. She had been the anchor of their family. Like all families, when you lose your mother it hits a particular nerve and a special type of sorrow. She was a good mother and she was a good wife. We all loved her very much. The grand children especially took it hard, she had been a baby sitter for most of her children's children and raised them the same as she did her own children. They loved her for her understanding and her compassionate concerns for their happiness and well being. I felt the pain for the family at a time such as this. My wife took it hard, I tried to encourage her in every way that I could. The truth is, there is nothing that a person can do to stop the pain that you suffer when a situation like this occurs. This is something that only wears down in due time. Each person deals with this in their own way. Some take it better than others, but it does not mean that they are not hurt just as badly as the others, it only mean they dealt with it in their own way. There were many suits filed against the ship builders from people all across the country. Many had contracted the lung disease from the asbestos. The suit was won by the Attorneys from the U.S. Attorney's general office. The family received a small settlement. No amount of money could bring her back, nor could it stop the pain that they, the family had suffered.

This is the moment of truth for the family, now they had to put in to practice what their mother had been teaching them all time. Coming together, unifying the family and helping one another. All share the pain of each other and helping the younger ones to cope with the tragedy. Older ones took up more of the responsibilities. This is what their mother requested them to do. Most parents know that their time on earth is coming to an end. Soon or later, children have to take up the teachings of their parents and carry on with their lives. Many families have the tendency of straying away from the things that they had been taught by their parents while growing up to adult hood. There has to be a stern hand to try to keep them on the correct course. Most of the children had a family of their own; they had a hard job ahead of them. They had help to care for their young brothers and sister, while taking up some responsibilities in their own family. The family stayed together, worked together and did what their mother had asked them to do. Now they all were grown up and took on the responsibilities of an adult. They all had started their own families. Each anniversary of her death, the children and grand children go to the cemetery to pay respect and place flowers on her grave. As I had mention before, when tragedy strike in your family, each member has to deal with it in their own way. When I lost my father many years ago, I didn't go to the cemetery to visit his grave. I loved him very much; I always loved him and adored him from the time I ever knew him. If I would visit his grave on an annual basis, I would not be able to function. It would bring back too many memories. There is not a day that goes by that I am not thinking about him. He will always be by hero. I wanted to be just like my father. The man I knew was every thing that you could ask of a father, a husband and a just man. I rather remember him as I do, not going to the cemetery and feeling sad or sorrow in my heart. Father had lived a good life and had done what God had asked of him to do. Now his reward is in heaven. I feel good and confident that this man is in Heaven.

My two youngest children never had any children. For what ever reason for them not having children is their personal choice. Carla was a career wife, perhaps she thought she would not be able to pursue her dreams when tied down with children. Michael never had any children either, again the reason is not known why, perhaps he to do not want the responsibilities of having children, besides he never got married. He said he never found the right woman for him to marry. We all make choices in life, some don't necessary have to agree with our way of thinking, but this is the choice that they made and they would have to live with that choice. Michael had skills in most sports, but he never tried to play in any of the major professional leagues. He was contented in having a decent job and a place to live. I would have wanted him to at least try to play for any of the professional sports. He had the size to play any of the sports; he is six feet six inches tall and weighs nearly two hundred and ninety pounds. He would have been a good foot ball player, basket- ball, and a good baseball player. He could have been a good heavy weight fighter. These sports did not appeal to him on a professional scale. He was good in all of these sports. However, he did play these sports in high school. Carla, the baby girl was just the opposite of Michael, she would tackle any sport. She played basket ball, volley ball, tennis and other sports that were open to girls. Carla, was also a career minded person, she pursued a modeling career and in fashion. She later went into the medical analyst field, there she made her career. She married and had no children. A few years had gone by and everyone seems to be coming back to normal. Then sickness came up on my wife's oldest brother. Cornell had been diagnosed with a bad heart and his arteries had begun to close up on him. He had to get the arteries cleaned and routed as soon as he could. They had to give him four by passes to his heart. This was devastating to the family, having to go through another tragedy in the family. He received the by-pass and was doing well in recovering. He went for six years without any complications. Then he began to have shortness of the breath and tired out very easily. A few more years passed by and his condition began to worsen, his activities were limited and the food that he ate were screened.

Cornell, had always been a strong individual, he had been in the U.S. Marines and took the best that they threw at him. He came through all the training and other things that he had to endure in the Marines, and he had broken many track records, set track records in schools that still stand to this day. No one would have ever suspected him out of all the children to have a problem with his heart. He did physical labor on the job that he had in civilian life. He was a welder for a railroad yard and a ship yard. He liked to fish for his pleasure. Him and I used to go fishing some times and he enjoyed being on the fish bank. He still holds the record for the largest big mouth bass that was ever caught between him and me. The bass was caught in the Columbia River and it weighed five pounds. This truly was a large fish, the largest bass that I have ever seen caught, big or small mouth. Cornell was also good in football, basketball, track, and baseball. He was a rugged participant and played with great skill. This is why it was so hard to talk about his sickness. Sickness don't discriminate, any one or any thing can be over come by this enemy of life, Cornell passed on, now the family was once again in sorrow, a few years earlier, they had lost their mother. Cornell had been a strong force in keeping his family together after his mother had passed away, now the whole family had to be stronger and more united than ever. The son-in laws had to do what ever they could to try and keep the boys in line with what Cornell would have wanted for them. After their father had passed away, Cornell was looked upon as being the man of the family and the leader of the children that were left behind. They all loved Cornell and respected his advice. It seems if though the good is the ones that pass on first. May be their job on earth have been completed and God had no other mission for him to full-fill in this life. The journey through life is truly a journey of a relay. We all travel so far in life, and then we pass the baton off to another member, hoping that they would carry on to the finish line. Many of us fall down along the way, but jump back and continue the race.

The death was truly a big tragedy, and each family member had to deal with it in their own way. The sorrow and the hurt that we all encountered had to wear it self off in due time. We all have gotten through other deaths in our families; it is never easy, helping one another in a sorrowful situation to calm the pain. There should be something good to say about each person that passes through life and into another. Just living on earth in this life, is a big challenge to man kind, sin is all around us. We are constantly be tempted by things that will sap your soul and put you on a pass to" meet Lucifer in his designated place" When we work hard in trying to avoid" Lucifer's snare." It is an impossibility to walk this walk alone, there has to be a stronger force that guides us. It has to be the Spirit of God that guides and direct us in the right direction, so when people leave this life, we hopefully, will go to a better place. The average person goes through" hell here on earth", they should not end up in another in the life after this one. Yet the" Bible tells us that it is not God's will that any of us should perish, and for us all to have everlasting life". God gave us all a way out of hell. By serving him and keeping his commandments, we can avoid the everlasting hell. We should live a life on earth that will reflect the type of person that we try to be. We all should leave a good legacy behind us when we leave this life. No one should be put in a position of having to say things about the deceased that will be contradictory to their life style. If you cannot say anything positive about the deceased, then it would be better for you not to say anything. Life should be lived to make people want to talk about and say positive things that you accomplished in this life. We all could feel good about telling the truth about the deceased and their life. All of us like to say good things about people when they passes on, it's not in our culture to ever say anything negative about a person when they passes on to the other side. There are many reasons for us never to talk negative about an individual; one reason is; only God knows where this person will end up. The Bible says," there will be people in Heaven that you thought would go to hell, and there would be some people that is going to hell that you thought would go to Heaven". The final judgments will come from God and he look at the heart of man. The grace of a Good God will be the measuring stick.

I often wonder what was my father trying to say to my mother, when he was lying flat on the top of the stairs to the up-stairs hall way. Mother said that he was trying to tell her something, the words never came out, but his lips were trying to say something. Mother is puzzled until this day, what it was that he was trying to say to her. We will never really know, but the speculation is he was trying to tell her, this was the end of his life on this earth. He could have told her that he loved her and he would see her over on the other side. He could have said to tell all of his children good by, and to take care of mother. All of these things we would like to think that he was trying to relay on to her. Time ran out and it never was made clear on just what he was trying to say to mother. The hero in my life was gone, it would have been good to know what he was trying to say, but nothing would erase the pain and hurt that we had experienced in his passing. This is not a monopoly on pain and suffering, I am sure that any one that loses some one in their family has gone through the same feeling that we received in our father passing away. How many people can be glad when their love one passes on? And how many people will be sad when a new born is brought into this world? as hard as it might seem, the Bible say this is what we should do. We weep when they come into this world, and we are supposed to be glad when they leave. It is only human nature for us to do the opposite. The Bible speaks of man born by woman; days are few and full of trouble. The difference is, born of flesh, versus being born by the spirit. We all need to be re-born the second birth is by the Spirit of God. I can talk boldly about the power of God and his mercy. Many years ago I experienced the love and the mercy of God. I knew from the beginning of my life, I had been asked for by my father. He had prayed to God for a son, and his prayers were answered. I am the product of his prayer. Father used to tell me that he had asked God for a son and keep him well and safe until he would be ready to take him back. I, like other young men, had an urge to experience life on the other side. Father told me that I was a special son and if I went too far out into the world, then God would chastise me in one way or the other. His predictions came true, I was chastised on many occasion. I had gotten a little too far out into the world. I knew what was right and I knew what was wrong, I had been taught constantly by my parents to do the right thing and to stay out of trouble. I did things that were against their teachings and suffered some of the consequences of disobedient. I used to chase after women, started to drink alcohol on a part- time basis, going to the race track and other things that were against the teachings. I wanted to be with the boys, go out and spurt the town; we even went across the State line to Washington, just to see friends that we had met in Portland. I had become a disobedient child to some extent. Years later, I was put back on the right track of life by a bullet that nearly took my life.

Many of these things that took place in my secret life were never known about in my family. One night after working a part time security job, a party was given at a girl's house that I had gone to school with. Her friends were invited. Jack, my long time school friend had invited me over to her house, and I accepted the invitation and dropped by after work, they had alcohol and every one seem to be having a good time. My mistake was, I stayed there too long and came home with the smell of alcohol on my breath. Wife began to draw conclusions, she accused me of two- timing her and that I was not faithful to her. I was faithful to her doing our marriage, my chasing girls came before we were married. Once we were married I became a family man and was devoted to my family. However, her perception of me not being faithful to her was instilled in her mind. When I came home, I went straight to the bed room to un- dress the security uniform that I wear on the security job. In taking my pistol belt and pistol off from around my waist, the wife came in and brandishing a 22-caliber automatic pistol, this pistol that we had around the house was for safety, and to take hunting with me as a back up weapon during hunting season. This weapon was loaded always, I thought the safety on, the wife pointed the weapon in my direction to try and frighten me, and she did just that. I was frightened by her pointing the hair trigger pistol in my direction; I knew she did not know anything about a weapon and especially this one. It had a hair trigger, and with the safety being off, it would take a small jolt to fire it. Well, the un-thinkable thing happened, the thing that I was hoping would not happen, the pistol went off and struck me in my neck on the left side, only missing my juggler vein no more that one fourth of an inch. I felt a sensation of burning in my neck, and then the blood began to gush out of the wound. The wife went in shock and crying, wondering what she had done. She cried out that" it was an accident, and she did not know the weapon was loaded." I had to get to the hospital in a hurry, I was losing too much blood sitting there doing nothing. I wrapped my neck with a white bath tile and drove my self up to the Kaiser hospital. It was after hours and the doors were locked. The security guard that was on duty came to the door and let me in. The hospital's staff saw what had happened to me and rushed me into the operating room. I had begun to blank out after a while, but still conscious. They placed me on the operating table, examined the wound and clamped the wound so it would not bleed; I had lost much blood before I got to the hospital. The whole family had come to the hospital to see what had happened, and pray for my recovery. The doctors told me that" I was the luckiest person that they had ever seen. He said the bullet had barely missed my juggler vein. He said someone was watching over me", he didn't see how I survived a wound such as that. The bullet entered through the left side of my neck and followed my jaw bone along my left cheek bone and out of my chin. The bullet had left my body and lodged in the wall. The police came and investigated the incident. They wanted to know what happened, and if I wanted to press charges. I responded to that question by saying no. I didn't think that she tried to fire the weapon; I only think she wanted to frighten me. The weapon discharged and struck me in the vital area. I had no doubt that it was an accident. Still without God sparing my life, I could have been just as dead as if it was on purpose. I believe this was a warning from God, he was telling me to straighten my life and to change my lifestyle. My wife was in sorrow for many months, although I was up and recovering at a un- heard of pace. This is one of the reasons for me to say boldly, that God is a good

James L. Bryant, Jr.

God and his mercy is with us. Some times he has to get our attention by allowing things to happen to us that are not so pleasant. My father had warned me of what would happen if I strayed to far out into the world. If this had not happened, I could not tell how far I would have ventured out from the teachings of my Christian parents.

Chapter Eight

I had two obligations that I had to live up to. The first thing is, I was asked for by my father from God, and the second thing is, I asked God for a mate, some one that I could be true to and love as my own. I had seen what was out in the world; there were nothing out there that I wanted to spend the rest of my life with. Things out there were all short lived. I asked for a long time partner, a true mate, some one to raise a family with. Some where along the way, I became side tracked and ventured out into a place for me being where I was supposed to have been. Mother knew the wrath of God had come upon me for my straying off the main course of life. Every one gave us encouragement to pick up the pieces and continue with our lives. My life had been spared for a reason. Prayer and a promise from God were in the working. I am glad that my life was spared, and I learned a strong lesson from the un-fortunately incident. I know that we all have something in our lives that we would never talk about, as long as people don't know about them, then why tell them. My situation was different; I was exposed to the family by my loose living. I have prayed for and placed into God's hand by my parents. When I did not measure up to expectations, then I was subjected to consequence. I learned much about going against the grain. My second encounter with death was in the Pacific Ocean. My uncle and aunt had invited me to go ocean fishing with them, uncle had a huge boat that he pull behind his G. M. C pick up truck. We went to the sea resort town of Tillamook, Oregon. It was a beautiful, sunny day, with a slight wind, just normal for the coastal areas. We launched the boat and went out beyond the jetty; the water was calm and deep. Once we passed beyond the jetty, the ocean was so calm you did not notice that you were that far out there. Shortly after we cast our lines into the water and received a few big bites, the wind came up and the sea got rough. Uncle immediately, started the twin mercury engines up and we reeled in our lines, we then headed back to shore. The water was so rough that we had doubts if we would get back to shore. The waves were very high and when the swells came in, the boat would rise ten or fifteen feet into the air. When the waves would go down, it seems if you were going to hit the bottom of the ocean. This was a time of truth. I prayed to God to spare us to get back to the shore safely. I said that I would" never" get back into the ocean on a boat. God blessed us to get back to the shore safely, but had fear of ever going out into the ocean on a boat to catch fish. However, I did fish from the jetty rocks in the bay.

There was a third time that I had experienced trouble on the waters. We used to go fishing in a huge lake on the southern Oregon coast, this was a fresh water lake and it was deep and wide. The huge lake had many species of fresh water fish and some striped bass that come up from the ocean. The lake was on the left side of the highway, about 2 miles from the ocean. There were many rivers and lakes in southern Oregon. There were some that ran into the ocean. Some species of fish could live in both, salt and fresh water. The bass would use the fresh water lake to spawn. These were huge fish; you would have to use a heavy duty reel to land them if you were lucky enough to catch one. We used a long under- powered boat to go out into the lake in, again the water was calm, beautiful sunny day and there were no signs of any storm coming in. We went out about three miles and started to fish, we were fishing for anything that would bite our bait, there were fish being caught. We were catching big and small mouth bass, trout, crappies, blue gills, perch and some catfish. Then the wind came up, the clouds began to come and soon it turned dark and foggy, we had to pull the anchor up and head back to the shore. I didn't think that we were going to make it back to the shore. There were three boats with three people per boat. All the boats were experiencing the same ordeal. The waves began to come from all sides; they rammed against the boats and slowed the forward progress of our trying to reach the shore line. We could barely see the shore from where we were. The fog was getting heaver and more dense, the waves were having it way with our under- powered boat. We did not have enough horse power to ride over the waves before there would be more coming from the opposite direction. We had to use a gallon bucket to throw water out of our boats; this was a slow and fearful experience, being at the mercy of the lake. It took us twice as long to get back to shore as it did for us to come out this far. When we finally got back to shore, we went to the owner of the marina and asked him, why he rent us a big boat with little horse power? The owner said he did not know what the horse powers of the motors on the boats were.

Again, we had to give praise and thanks to God for bringing us through the angry waters. There were many other times that I could have been killed or seriously injured. There were times when I was driving the bus for the transit system and a small voice would say for me to wait a few seconds, being at the red light and the light was in my favor, I hesitated to go for a few seconds. Some one barrels through the red light traveling at a high speed, if I had not hesitated for those few seconds, I would have been broad sided, passengers or myself could have been killed or seriously injured. There have been other close encounters with possible death or serious injury. When I say things about the Goodness of God and his mercy, then I talk about knowledge of his love and mercy for me. When I see people that have died from accidents, injuries and other causes that were less injured than I have been, and did not come through, I have to give God all the praise and all the glory. There is no man that can save himself, you can try to do everything in your power to stay safe but if God is not there to bring you through these situations, there would not be any escape. I know that my time is coming when God will say that your time here on earth is up, I hope I am ready to go with him when he comes for me. He said that our time here on earth is short and full of trouble. We all would like to be around as long as we could, but we do not hold the key to life and death. Only God have jurisdiction over both our bodies and our souls. There seem to be so much that he has to say about his life, how he has been blessed, the close encounters with bodily harm or even death, the journey that you have traveled through this life, the good, bad and ugly experiences through life. You would like for everyone to feel the fullness of information that you would pass on to others. I know that we all have a story to tell, if you have traveled through life to the point of where I am in life, I am sure that there are many stories that could be told about your journey. It seems if though there is too much I want to say to others, to try to contain the information within myself.

My desire to want to write something, whether it would be fiction or facts came at an early age of ten or eleven years old. I have read the stories of many writers, those who told of their true life stories. These writers had a compelling desire for me to tell others how my life was, the place where I was born, the segregation in the south, schools that I had gone to, friends that I left behind, the ancestors and their dedication to staying the course. Looking at an ever changing world. All of this is points of interest to me I would like for my children and my grand children to look back at my life, how I was raised and grew up to become a family man myself, and my heroes, my parents was the biggest influence in my life. There could not be enough said about them. My grand parents, who stood fast and never gave up, were a strong instrument in my life also. When I first had the urge to write about my journey through life, I decided to bar nothing in my experiences and my feeling toward the situation in this world and my surroundings. I would tell it as I see it, or the experiences that I had witnessed. I know we are not living in a perfect world; we never have and probably never will live in a perfect world, but there is much that we can do to make it a better place to live. I believe the first thing would be to eliminate greed, sharing more of the world's wealth with people less fortunate than our selves, education to people that is not up to the present time. Punish the thieves and robbers that take away from the less fortunate people of our world. This world was created with every thing that man or animal needed to survive on. All the plants and other life sustaining materials were already put in place here on earth and in the sea before we were created. We only had to be good stewards of what was placed here by our creator. The spirit of greed came into the picture; man wanted more and more of the world's wealth. Certain nations and certain individuals, wanted every thing for themselves, leaving their fellow man kind in need of the bare necessities of life, the land that grows the food have been monopolized, the natural resources have been taken by a few greedy nations or individuals. The reality is most of the poverty in the world is caused by man's action against man. His intent is to control and keep these people dependant on them and not independence. Most of the poverty in the world today could be minimized if we did not have greedy people taking more than what is needed to survive. What can one person do with hundreds of millions of dollars? And there are others that have nothing or very little. Do you think that this was the act of God, or the greed of man that created these situations? My belief is that men caused these problems.

Not all rich people is the same, there are some that want to right the world's problems, they give large sums of money, time and materials to help people and nations to come out off poverty. In our own country during the slavery years, there were wealthy people that helped the slave cause. There were many that were greedy and wanted nothing but more and more of what ever there were to turn a profit. Were this type of thinking taught to us by our ancestors or was it something that we developed on our own? What ever the reason for our greed, the world has began to look at our problems in a different light. They have begun to realize that greed is the basis of nearly all of our world's problems. The nations of the world have come together and try to solve most of the basis problems. Every human should have the necessary things of life. These rights are; food, health, shelter and an opportunity to achieve their dreams. I have witnessed inequality, segregation, discrimination and injustices to Black people. In the southern states, there were laws on the books to keep you from achieving these goals. You had to abide by them, regardless of how unjust they were. We had to use the second time around on everything. Even some of the clothing that you wore was hand downs, things that someone else had worn before you had received them. The books that we had to study in were hand me downs. When the white students did not have any more use for them, they would be brought over to the Black schools. These tactics always keep the Black students at least one or more grades behind the white students. These were all facts about the un-just system that we were forced to live under. Never less, these same people that called themselves" God fearing Christians", were the same people that kept the Black race down. As long as you would show to be two or three steps below them and remained there, then they were satisfied with you. This is another case of them not wanting the Black people to become independent, but to stay depending up on them. When they saw a well educated Black that spoke well and had knowledge, they would say he was too uppity. They could not see someone that they had tried to keep down from having knowledge of his surroundings, could talk on the same level with them. As time went by, more Blacks were going to college and universities. They had fought the fight on their own terms. We have not won the fight yet, but we continue to gain ground. The young people of this country will be the ones that will change the ways the older people used to do business Young Blacks and Whites who want something different in our land of opportunity. Some of the older people would like to turn back the hands of time to where it had been four hundred years ago, they still teach their children to "hate and to avoid people of other races"They had been taught that they are God's special race of people and that he gave them all of the power to rule over every other race of people". We the Black people have been told for too long that we were inferior to them. Some Blacks even think of it in that way, blacks have been brain washed and can't seem to think any other way, the White race has done a good job in teaching" hate and separation between the races". To this day, they still proclaim to be God fearing Christians. The young people of this world will be the ones that will put things on a better footing for the whole world.

Four hundred years of traveling toward justice, equality, and opportunities is becoming closer as each generation jumps into the race. The world is getting smaller; we are no longer an island unto ourselves. Technology, communication, trade, and an exchange of information between nations are essential for us to make a better world for all. This is not just for a few who think the world was created only for them. The older people have made a mockery out of Christianity. They have told the rest of the world that how "God fearing and Christian they are", and living just the opposite. There have been some White people that try to live the Christian life, but the majority of them still live just the opposite of what they teach. You only have to look at history and find the truth about their self- proclaimed Christianity. The political issues seem to be more important than the practice of the true faith. When a father sends his son to school and having hate symbols and hate messages printed all over his tea shirt, then there is something to be said about the true faith of this individual. Old hatred die hard, it took four hundred years to get to this point and it will take a long time to get this out of the minds of those who harbors hate in their hearts. Black people have suffered much through this constant practice of discrimination. This practice will not help any cause.

There have been many gains made by Blacks, we cannot deny this, many people who gave their lives and beaten, thrown in jail for no reason except to reveal the in-justices that exists. Both, Whites and Blacks have lost their lives for the just cause. They were the people that set the pace and way for us to keep marching forward. In the twenty -seven years that I worked for the transit system, I experienced some discrimination from the passengers that I served. When I was employed as a fare inspector, I was checking fares aboard the newly constructed light rail system I walked down the isle of the train that I was on, checking for proof of fares. I came across this elder White male and ask him for his proof of fare, the elderly gentleman looked at me and said "he would not show me anything" I wanted to know the reason why, everyone else were cooperating and he did not. 'I wondered if I had said anything that I should not have said", there were nothing that I had said or done for him not to want to cooperate. "The gentleman said that he would not show me his ticket, but would show it to my partner who was a White person" The train pulled into the gate way transit station, there we asked the gentleman to de-board the train. My partner then wrote the citation for refusing to show his proof of fare upon a request from the fare inspector. It was evident that the elderly gentleman did not like Black folks. This was the first time that I had a White person to out-right refused to cooperate with me because of my race. The second time I had an incident like this, was patrolling the train's platform, a young White boy that had been walking up and down the platform, looking for an opportunity to jump on the train and get a free ride. As long as the inspectors were watching him, he would not try to board the trains when they arrived at the station. I had been watching him for about a half of an hour. I then approached him and asked to see his proof of fare. He said that he did not have one and that he was waiting for some one. We asked him to leave the platform if he was not to board the train. He then said a smart word. He said "this was the reason why he could not get a job, and that you people have gotten all of the jobs" he did not come out completely and say what he wanted to say but enough to let me know how he feel toward minorities and say he thought too many Blacks having too many good jobs and that was the reason, but he gave the impression of not wanting to see Blacks in good high paying jobs. There were other incidents that involved my race in a position of authority. However, I had no problems with the people that were over me. I was asked to put in for a lead fare inspector, but I only had a few years to go before I would retire, I refused the request to put in for the position. I re-tired in a few years after that. I have been re-tired every since. With so much spare time on my hands, other re-tire had seen the same thing that I had witnessed in my dealing with the public. We had seen a need for some one to come to the rescue of all these young people that had no since of direction, they were just out in the streets, no place to go but in the streets, never knowing where their next meals were coming from or where they would lay their heads. Some were put out of their homes, others left on their own, but what ever the reason, the kids were still in the streets and needed guidance. We formed a club to help the ones that wanted and needed our help. After a few meetings together, we began to get through all of the formalities in order, and chose a title for our club. We had many suggestions on what title or name of the club. The decision was made to use the name of "true dialogue", this was a fitting name for our club, and this is what we had hoped to do, have true dialogue with the ones that we would be trying to help. We received requests to come to parents home to talk to their wayward child, come to schools to try and mentor some un-motivated students. We later joined forces with the Urban League of Portland. They had all the contacts with the schools that had need for assistance. Our club still exists and is progressing.

The truth has to be told, regardless of who it may hurt. When something is said about an individual, race, group or nation, sometime bad feelings occur. But if you are a clear minded individual, nation, race or group, and you can hear the truth, and then you will accept what I am trying to say to you. The truth is the only thing that will stand for eternity. A lie may sound good to your ears, and might make you feel good for a time, but the truth will eventually come out. The truth is not always pleasant to hear, and sometimes the truth hurts, but a lie will hurt you in time worse than the truth. In my race there are many things that we, as a race can do to improve our lives. We have to stop allowing bad things to take place in neighborhoods, our communities, calling the shots as they really are, stopping drugs, prostitution and killing up one another. If we want the rest of society to give us the respect that we want, we have to take the responsibilities of our communities, those that are able to work and hold down a job, should be working and contributing to a better tomorrow for our young ones. Give them something to be proud off. Teach them about our history and how far we have come to make the gains in life that we now have. Let them know that what freedoms that we do have, came at a price. Both, White and Black people came together to argue, march, die, beaten, and jailed for our progress. Nothing was automatically given to us. There were dedicated fore-runners that had paved the route for us to travel. There are many obstacles to overcome yet, but we should never be complacent. Keeping the dreams alive, the ancestors of yesteryear could only hope for a better tomorrow for their children. They knew that they would not see the dream that they had hope for their children, but they knew that God would answer their prayers in his own time and things would make a change. God's time is not our time, we cannot rush God to come quickly and do what we want him to do in our time schedule. He may not come when you want him to come, but he is always on time. Everything under the sun has a season to act out, or carry out what has been spoken of, again Prayer and patience is the key to our wants and our needs If these things are in God's will. To deny the power of God is not being realistic. There are too much evidence around us to deny his truth and his power. We pray for what we want him to do in our lives and hold on.

There has been much progress made by our people. We only hear and see the negative things in our lives that is exposed and talked about on the national news. There are many young people going to school beyond the high school level. Some are in trade schools, some are in law school, medical school and many more educational establishments. These young people should be given much credit in their accomplishments. This is another way to let the less motivated students to see that it can be done and this should be a motivator for others to follow. They only need to apply themselves and work toward their goals. We now have Senators, Reps., Governors, congressmen, and other high positions of the Government. We have many top ranked military personnel. We have captains, majors, colonels, and top ranking Generals. There are top security personnel; we are in all phases of Government. We also have some high positions in private establishments. You could say one of the most visible signs is we can see the first Black President nominee that has ever gone this far into a selection of the next President of the U.S. this is truly progress in the making. Hopefully, he will win the white house and become the first of any race other than a White man. The road is not easy for him; the opposition has thrown everything that they possibly could throw at him in hopes of de-railing his campaign. They have lied, deceived, and twisted the truth, investigated and many other things to try to de-rail him. He seems to be getting stronger in quest for the Presidency. It is my belief that God is again in this plan, He has brought along many leaders to guide us out of our situation. Each one He had chosen to run this race completed the portion of the race that he or she was assigned to run. He had people's hearts changed to help those who ran this race. There are many that think the first Black President hopeful, is up to the task and ready for the change that the world so urgently need

Americans who is helping his campaign in many ways; money, votes and their assistance to his campaign. My parents would have never dreamed of a Black President. Now their children are seeing a great possibility of this happening. This would truly be a story to be told through out the generations to come. A descendant of slaves, make it to the Presidency, up from the ashes to a beautiful circumstance. This is a story to be told through out the world. The most powerful nation on earth is run by a descendent of slaves. This is what those old ancestors could only think of how it could be. Records of all kinds have been set or broken; he has galvanized people of all races, groups, persuasions and religions to join his march for a change in the way the world do business.

If it were not for the few greedy people of the world, there would be more to go around for all. It would not be hungry people, people who don't have a place to sleep. Those that have families would have a house to raise their families in. They would have access to health, hospitalization, and other medical care. This is the evils that men have imposed upon men. The will to be conquers, rulers and to be the dominant forces in man's life. These people don't want you to sell, buy, or trade without them being at the top of the scale. If you don't jump to their desires, they will impose sanctions upon you. Medicine will be withheld from the people that need it most. The truth is the world will do nothing for any other nation unless there is something in the gift for them. Some less-fortunate nations sell their natural resources, there land and any thing else of value to acquire the basis necessities of their nation, eyes are being open to what has been going on for centuries. Things have now begun to catch up with the culprits of the world. The world needs a major change, and the young people of all the nations of the world will be the ones that will institute the change. The ones that are just now trying to catch up with technology will have to go back to school and re-educate themselves, or they will be left behind while the rest of the world passes them by. We need to up-grade our manufacturing abilities so we can keep the good paying jobs here in the U.S., we should become good stewards in keeping our air clean. Don't just think of profit, if we continue to contaminate the planet that we live on, and then we all will perish for the sake of a few greedy people that put profit before the well being of its inhabitants. A change is coming, and the future of our planet depends upon the young and future generations. We have raped the land of many resources, diamonds, oil, gold, plutonium, and ores of all kinds. We have raped the sea, killing many species of marine life, disturbing the food chain, over harvesting the main source of food for many nations.

There is no doubt that we all have benefited to some extent in what has taken place on our planet. But the big profits come from a few; we sell our birth rights to these greedy ones that do not have our well being in mind. They are looking for one thing only, and this is profit at any cost and at anyone expense. Practices such as these will have to cease if we are to have a better world, a world of the haves and the haves not. The margin should be closer between nations of the world. The reality is that the people with much more than what they need to survive comfortably, is not willing to give up their billions to help the ones that is in poverty. They forget, man's greed is the cause of eighty five- percent of the world's poverty. Some nations have given their technology and materials to some un-developed nations and tried to make a difference in their lives. And there are others who would not give, but to take everything that they could take from them. When they give help to these people, they charge them an arm and a leg; they would be indebted to them for many decades to come, and leaving the next generation of people still indebted. These people would never come from under the umbrella of debt. This is the way that they keep these nations in poverty. It is a way to keep them dependant upon them and never allowing them to become independent. Everything that they would ever need would have to come through them. I have read many books on why nations are impoverished, nearly all got this way because of greed. This greed either come in by two ways, the nations that are guilty of these practices are the ones that try to keep it people from achieving, keeping them depending on their government for all of their needs. This is the way they exercise control over its people. Another way is to sell out to another country or nation; these governments sell out to other nations. They are promised a good living and many other materialistic gains. These countries also become a nation of poverty. The people are always the ones that suffer from these practices. Nations that won't cooperate with the aggressors will have their leadership replaced in whatever way that the greedy aggressors deems necessary. Some time it is a replacement of the leader with someone else that is more to their liking, or it might be death. The power that these aggressors have over another nation is remarkable. Most people know nothing what is taking place. There is corruption in every phase of our existence. It is in our churches, schools, police, and jobs in industry and in government. If only it could be possible for our ancestors to see all of the accomplishments that we have gained, they would be very pleased. We know that the race is not completed, but we have the will to keep running. The American people know the time has come to make a change, those who want a better future for the future generations is on board to make a better tomorrow for all. A massive clean up in our government is needed to punish the corrupt and the greedy ones, that have kept us back as a people and as a nation. The priorities have to be changed, old prejudices and hate that have hurt us as a nation and as a people. A new day is fast approaching, there will be some that will stop at nothing to try and derail the progress that has been made. If the people of this country can make huge metropolis out of the forest, the desert and the mountain side, then there is nothing that cannot be accomplished if we are on one accord. Those who oppose progress need a renewing of their minds. They cannot continue to do business as usual. The whole world is changing and they might as well come aboard and join the ranks of the future powers. This is not the time to dwell on the past, things happened at that time and place in history that we had no control over, but it will play out its role in history just like everything else. It is true, our past is nothing to be proud off, but we have made many gains that you can be proud off. The older citizens of our country should not try to stop progress by teaching hate and separation between other races or groups. They should exercise their" Christian faith in line with what the Bible teaches them to do". This seem to be a very hard thing for some of the really "die harden citizens" to do. They seem to rather live in the past than face the future. A selfish way of thinking, but it is true.

These people have to realize that they need to communicate with other people of the world. They are no longer an island unto themselves.

Growing up on my grandfather's farm, I use to see him relax on the front porch after plowing his crops all day, sitting on an old swing, reading a old news paper that was two or three weeks old. The paper was a current events paper that had three weeks of old news in it. This is the time that made me feel good, seeing him with a corn cob pipe in his mouth. I often wondered what was on his mind. Maybe it was his crops, his animals, his children or the future of his race. What ever it was, he never let it interfere with life or his family's life. He kept doing what he usually does for years in and years out.

We have to give all the respect that we can to our ancestors. They came through one of the tough times in human history. They survived the beating, lynching, discrimination and other atrocities against them. They could not tell the truth about questions that were asked them. They could not exercise any part of their man hood, they had to say no sir, and yes master to the questions that were put before them. They had been forced to act this way if they wanted to survive. God was in their corner and he guided them to where we are today. They had God to depend upon, and trusted him to bring them through the difficult times in our history. We were a people in the making; we had to go through all these difficult times in order for us to reach this point in our long history. No other people have endured so much and still had love in our hearts. We have never tried to over throw or rebel against the government. We remain loyal to the country. We are one of the most loyal people in this country. We have fought and died for the country, in hope that one day things would be different. Our ancestors never did see the seeds that they had planted to materialize, but their patience and prayers are the evident of where their children are today. We cannot forget how far we have come, the suffering of the forebears to plot a course for us to pursue. None violent was a proven way to go. Although there were freedom or death cried out on many occasion, there were restraint in the ranks. The ministers were the holding force behind them. Today that same spirit and guidance is in the Black communities. Respect is given the man of God; ministers were the most dominant force in the community. As time went by, more of us had a desire to break away from what has gotten us to this point. We had nothing, no power, and no say in our lives. We only did what we were told to do and say what we were told to say. We didn't have any kind of rights or say in how we were being treated. We were reduced to no more than one of the animals that were on the farm. We were considered to be only a fraction of a man. The same mentality among some exists today.

Uncle Henry passes on: one of father's last remaining brothers passed away. He was the youngest to my father. He is one of the reasons for us moving to Portland. Many years before we came out west, Uncle Henry had already been established in a job and a house for his family. He worked hard, holding down a full and a part- time job. His part-time work would be to haul scrap iron and sell it to the various scrap yards. He earned good money in hauling scrap iron. He was a funny man, he liked to make jokes and have fun, he had a speech problem when he tried to make a long sentence, and sometimes he could barely get his words out. Uncle Henry had this problem from birth, but the people that knew him could understand him and knew what he was trying to relay to them. He had a large family, four boys and five girls. They had a big house that they lived in on Mississippi on the north part of town. He was a good man that provided for his family. They were together all the years that he was married. He is missed by friends and family that knew him. His family is carrying on the love for each other that he had left behind for them to continue, helping one another, talking to the younger ones and try to be brothers and sisters to each other that he had instilled in them. He had been raised in a family that thought this was the only way to live. They were a close family in caring and helping one another, when one or more needed help. One day we all will be together again. There will be no more heart ache, no sorrow. It will only be joy, peace and harmony in the next life. If we hope to come together again, there are things that we must do to be accepted in a place like that. We have the rules and regulations that allow us to meet this goal.

We have been promised that we will leave this world and everything that is in it behind, we cannot take anything with us to the other life. Everyone that crosses over to the other side has to come alone, no one can take your place and no one can break their appointment. All of our emphasis should be on the after life. The Holy Bible states: what profits a man to gain the world and lose his soul? This is plainly said. So why should we do anything under the sun to accumulate material wealth? In the end, without Christ it all have been in vein. Only what you do to boost his kingdom will last. This is the reason for people not to be too serious about materialistic wealth. Prepare your self for the things to come. Heaven is our next home and we will be there for eternity. This is assuming all the people that profess to be Christians and God fearing people. There will be no hypocrites, gamblers, prostitutes; lies, thieves, or sin of any kind enter into Heaven. The journey that I am talking about is not measured in physical miles. The long journey is psychological and spiritual, breaking through the barriers that stand in our way to reach our spiritual destination. We have been programmed to think the way that society wants us to think. They do not want us to think for ourselves. What they say is for us to take it at face value and not raise questions of its moral and legal standings. In order for us to reach the other side of this life, we have gone through, walk around, and sometimes go over the obstacles that stand in our way. Our sights should be set on one thing and one thing only that is our destination at the end of this journey. We can easily be caught up in the affairs of this world and lose sight of where we are trying to go. At the end of our journey, we all would look back at the long journey and declare that we had run a good race, we had reached our destination and worthy of our reward. On this journey, we have encountered many kinds of obstacles that were in our way. There were deaths, sickness, discrimination, accusations and injustices. Sometime we were slowed down but never did we quit, never taking our eyes off our long journey. There were times that we slipped and slumbered. We regained our footing and proceeded on our way. There would be no mountain high enough, no river too wide to cross, no canyon too deep to keep us from our destination. This was the mentality of both, spiritual and our earthly walk through this life. In my life I have heard of all of the corruption in government, in our churches, our schools, communities and in our world. I have seen in news reels of Pastors, Bishops, and other men profess to love God, to do evil in the sight of God. Molestation, un- faithfulness, fornication and adultery had penetrated the ranks of leaders of the church. Confidence has been lost in these people to stand up and live the life that they tell their congregations to live. Only the strongest among men will survive this onslaught by the evil one. Mother has taken sick: sickness is the enemy of well being; death is the enemy of life itself. Yet each time that it comes, it always seem to be a new adventure to the family that suffers this tragedy. We can never adjust to it. We know that it is coming soon or later. We just don't know when, where or how, as mother often said: "be ready at all times, we don't know when the call for us to come home will come" always pray and ask God for forgiveness on every chance you have." we all have the same opportunity to be forgiven and saved by God as anyone else. Forgiveness and repentance is the things that we must do to be accepted in God's kingdom. Mother had fallen going up the basement stairs; she broke her arm and ruptured her hip. She went to the hospital, when my sister had been calling her house and never got a response. Sister became concerned and Brother Samuel went over to check on her, he found her at the bottom of the stair well, lying flat on her back, conscious but un-able to move. Samuel, immediately call for medical assistance and rushed her to the hospital. She had been diagnosed with injuries to her hip and a broken arm. This was a big blow to mother's life style, she was a very independent person and she never wanted to ask for any help. She had lived this way for many years after father had passed away. She would not give the house up and move in with any of her children. This is the home that God had given her and she would not leave there until God remove her. Years before the family had moved into this house, it was shown to her in a dream, the exact house in the exact area. This is why she was so appreciative to be in this house. God had placed her and her family in this house to live forever. She knew every crook and cranny in the house. Mother was satisfied to live alone in the house. She had the love of God to watch over her. Her enjoyment came from playing the piano, singing old hymns and giving God thanks for his love and mercy. Sometimes I would come over to the house and mother would be playing the piano and singing an old hymn. I had my key to the house, just as all of the children did. We would just open the door and come on in. Many times mother would not here us coming into the house, she would be in the spirit and not be worried about her surroundings. Other times she would be sitting in the dining room, reading the Holy Bible and praising God. This is the woman that I knew, always trying to perfect her self in the eyes of God. God had blessed her to see all of her children grow up to have families of their own and purchase homes for their families, and to see her grand children grow up and have families of their own. She was a great grandmother. This was why she praised God and trusted in him for her every need and desire. She trusted him for what she knew he can and would do when called upon him for her needs. She had much faith in God and put him at the forefront of her every desire and had no doubt that he would act in his own time. When you are around a person that is so filled with the Spirit of God, something radiates from them into you. You can feel the love of God all over them. You can tell if the spirit that is within them is real, no fake, this is all genuine and real feelings that she be experiencing and the spirit of God all around her. Anyone that would be near her at that time would have to feel the same Spirit. Maybe not to the extent that she is feeling at that time, but you had to feel some of the radiant power from around her come into you. She was thinking God for bringing her from a long way. From a small child on the farm, seeing no way out of their life style to where God had brought her to in that period of her life. She had come from a God fearing family and faith and belief was not a new thing in her life. All these values of good and evil were taught to her family at an early age and it was a thing that was taught to her children. All of her children had finished high school, all of her grand children had finished. Now her great grand children had finished and on their way to finishing up in Colleges and universities. She was thankful of seeing the power of God working in her family's lives. Two of the three girls that is in college, have majored in law and in medicine. They each have two years to graduate. This is something that father was not able to see. He had passed on many years earlier.

Chapter Nine

Mother passes on: this was and still is a major strike in our family and to everyone that knew her. She had lived the life that would assure her place in Heaven. Although it would be a great lost for the family and to the people that knew her and how she tried to live, would have no doubt of her receiving a place in Heaven. She left something behind that would make all of us proud. People, who did not know her personally, had heard much about her and wanted to pay their last respects to her. Her funeral services were over-flowing with well wishers and prayers for the ones that she had left behind. This is the type of life that a person wants to live, and leave behind for other people to speak highly and truthful about you when your life on earth has ended. The seeds that you plant in this life could touch people lives for many years to come. The deceased person won't know just how many lives are touched by the way that they lived their lives. This is one reason it is necessary to become a member of some church of your choosing. Everyone needs to be associated with the house of the Lord. We need close family ties, we need someone that we can come to and talk about our problems, the pastor for counseling if need be, and talking about the love of God. Experience taught me that being away from the house of the Lord is like being lost in a far away place. Coming home to people that love and communicate with you make you fell that family's culture. There is love and warmth in the house of the Lord that's not out in the world. This is where true love and caring for his fellow man will be. There is nothing like a person being made to feel like he or she is loved and cared about. Church will offer this feeling of family togetherness. Every one want to belong to someone or something, we were created to worship. The true worship is to worship God. If we don't know about him, then we are subjected to worshiping any idol god. God Almighty has instilled in all of us a certain degree of knowledge of Him we are a heads up on the evil things of this life. He gave human creation knowledge of right and wrong. We only have to exercise that right.

Since my childhood, I had a desire to want to express myself, to put into writing on how I feel and to tell of how my experiences in life had gone. There are too much to want to say to others, than keep it to my self. How I felt about life in the south, how my life was in the west. I wanted to relay the good, the bad and the ugly encounters of life and experiences. How mother prayed to see a better day for her family. I wanted to write about my father and my grand parents, my uncles and aunts, cousins, my sister and my brothers. I wanted to write about our immediate family, on how we grew up. This has always been my desire in this life. Now that I am older and have seen much, heard much and experienced much more. I am now in a position to write more about the journey. When I was young, I only had an urge to write. Now that I have gotten much older, I have gained more knowledge in writing a book on the long journey. Although, there are many people could write a story on their long journey through life, this is the journey of my life, as I know it. My journey is neither superior nor inferior to anyone else. This is what I gathered in life along my journey. The things have been true, the experiences that I have encountered, truths that I had been told, my personal feelings to situations in our world and in our country. The truth about our pass and the positive out-look for our future, the ever changing world that we live in the cooperation between the nations of the world, and the highly technological future of our world. There are so many positives in our future that it will over shadow all of the negatives that have occurred in our past. Many times we have to go back to the pass to see what were positives and what were negatives, we take the positive and improve upon it, and reject the negative, never to travel the negative ways again. The future generations should know all the things that took place in history, the truth should be told in giving this information, both the negatives things and the positives things that we as a people have encountered. The worst thing that we can do is to deny the truth. Not telling things the way they really were, and some of the things that still exists. Telling the truth is the only thing that will set us free from the lies. The truth hurt, a lie hurts even more. A lie that you would have to live with and your children lives with, does nothing to advance the cause of the future generations. The truth will set your mind free; you will feel a burden of guilt being lifted off your shoulders. We were created with a certain degree of right and wrong within our hearts, and when we don't exercise these truths, a burden of guilt is placed upon us. When things are off your conscious, you will feel a heavy weight being lifted off.

Two types of Christianity why are there two types of Christian worship? And why do some profess to be Christians live the opposite of what the definition defines Christianity to be? We all should know that Christianity represents being Christ like, and not like what we want it to be like. Again, we want to change the meaning of the word to fit our needs and our desires. This practice has kept us away from the truth, living a Christian life, takes discipline, control and truth. It is not a easy route to take, but if you are going to tell people of the world that we are Christians, and try to get them to do as we say do and not what the teachings say is expected of us, then we have missed the point. Christians know the struggle that they will have in trying to walk a straight line, and live up to the true meaning of being what is expected of them. True Christians have something that they can rely upon when they are faced with the temptations of this world. Only those who profess to be Christians in name only, have difficulty in being truthful in their thoughts and their deeds. The sooner that they can tell the truth about things in the past, the sooner they will release the burden of guilt upon their shoulders. A lie and living a lie is worse than the deeds that have been committed. Holding onto these un- truths is a burden on your conscious, hurt and to your professed Christianity. We all have sinned and came up short of what is expected of us, but when we know that we are in a state of denial, and refuse to admit our short comings, and then we are out in left field of where we profess to be.

Some older people have lived this lie for hundreds of years and still try to keep the lie alive by teaching the younger generation the same lie that they had been taught for years. We should not bear the burden of our fathers, many of them laid and passed the lie on to their love ones. These older ancestors were taught and programmed to keep the old tradition alive. Hopefully, the younger generation will become more aware of the wrong teachings that they had tried to instill into them. It is a hard thing to go against the old customs and teaching of your ancestors. But you should know the truth. The way to know this truth is to search for it reading, talking to other Christians and see where they stand on issues seeking knowledge to know the truth, through spiritual guidance.

When we read our history as a nation, we are not told the whole truth about our past. The books and other histories of our past will only expose that in which they want the generations to come know about. The truth about our reality will hurt and leave you in a state of doubt. There have been many creations and developments that were done by people that you have never heard off. These creations and developments were stolen from or bought off; therefore, their names would never show up in our history books. They like to show all the negative things that others contributed to our nation had done. All the positives had come from them and their ancestors. Truths are, many of these exposures were just the opposite of what they would have you to believe the way of past generations were to beat, steal, kill or any other means of getting what they desired. Divide and conquer, this was a practice of past generations. People of old were a selfish people; they did not want anyone to achieve and to make any progress, unless you were off their own racial and cultural back ground. This is the truths, it does not paint a pretty picture of our history, but the whole truth never does. This is the only thing that will last. My only hope is for the future generations to come can know the whole truth and build something positive from it. This way, as they go forward in trying to create a better world, they will know at what point in history that they could start from. Eliminate the lies and the negatives and rely upon the positives things in our history. I would like to see more people rely upon the true teaching of the Words of God. This is our measuring stick. Seek to find out what he wants us to do, and how he instructed us to live. These are the expectations of us from God. If we follow his desires and laws, we will not become deceived. I believe there is a difference in telling a lie, and constantly living a lie. A one time lie can be forgiven, if prayed for and repent from it, living a lie is constantly living the un-truths, a failure or a denial to even admit there is a lie. If the lie is not admitted, and not prayed for, and you continue to live in a state of denial without asking for forgiveness, then you are still living a lie and need repentance.

I have seen people that wanted something for nothing I have seen people that think that our government owes them everything. These people that think this way is a selfish people. They are looking for an excuse not to go out and try to do for themselves, this is their signal in saying that they want things free and did not want to hustle or work for what they want in life. Some want things to come easy for them. Some even think they deserve more than an opportunity to achieve, they wants a major head's start in accomplishing their goal in life. Our taxes help to support these people that have this kind of mentality. There will always be people that really need help, through no fault of their own, they came upon hard times. These are the ones that should be helped in desperate situations. Some have lost their jobs, the elderly and disabled. Un-able to meet the high cost of medical treatments and other legitimate causes to require public assistance. This is the way our taxes should be spent. Not to help the able body ones that just refuse to work and receive a pay check. Our society is made up of different kind of people, with different kinds of thoughts about who is responsible for their survival. One thing that is more important than others, this is an opportunity to progress in life, sometime we might need a helping hand to keep us moving forward, usually, this is a short time assistance. The one that is independent and not looking for a long duration of assistance will become independent as soon they get to that point. Each person should examine his own heart and find any thing there that would deny or take away from those that have the most need for assistance. Greed and selfishness should be eliminated from their desires. Too much of any thing is bad for the individual and bad for those who are in need of assistance.

My life would never be the same. I have worked with the rejected and displaced individuals in my work as a volunteer in the school system and working with people out in the streets. The stories that were told to me, by some, would make your heart melt. Young people put out of there homes and forced to live on the streets. Those that had some type of home to go to were in nearly as bad of circumstance as the ones without any place to go. Some were on the streets because of abuse by their parents or guardians. Others were put out of their parent's home, because of disobedience to their parent's rules and regulations. Yet there were some on the streets because of drugs and alcohol. All this seem to be a legal reason for them to be away from their parent's home. The fact is, these are children that need care and guidance. We all have a responsibility in trying to raise these children to become a good citizen in our world's society. It is my belief; many of these young people can be turned around and shown a more positive way in their lives. It takes much teachings and responsible adults to show them the right way to live their lives. Before this can happen, the people in question will have to want a better way of life for themselves. They will need to have their minds renewed, their thought process have to be changed. They have to see the change in people that is telling them what to do and how to act, on how they are living compared to what they are telling them to do. It is my belief that these people want help, and not wanting to live the life of a vagabond. Old friends that want nothing out life but their next drug fix or their next drink of alcohol will be the ones that will keep them from moving forward. There are two ways to go, if you are making progress in trying to live a more positive life style and your friends see the progress that you are making toward a change, and then you have the power to pull them up to the level in which you are trying to live. If you don't have a positive influence over their life, and they refuse to try to change their way of life, then it would be better to break away from these friends. The other way is that they will keep you in the same state of mind and on the same level with them. If you love your friends and care about the way his or her life is going, you should help them in every way possible, to help them in making a more positive change in their life. Let them know that you care for them very much, but their way of living is not pleasing to you and something has to done. Their friend ship has to be at a minimum. The way they are traveling is not in your plans for success. Some times it will be hard to say these words to some one that you have known for many years and have had close connection with. There are times that a hard decision has to be made by one who is trying to get their life on the right track. Nothing in our lives is so easy, that we can allow others to dictate which way that we will go. Choices are made by the individuals themselves. You can only, talk to, and try to live the example of the more positive life style. For a young mind, there are many distractions that will face them in life.

There are much hypocritical teachings to people in need for a change in their lives. We see this all over our society. Ones that is entrusted with the truth and the correct teachings to our love ones is not telling them the complete truths, they are telling them what will sound good to their ears and not what is good for their lives. A few examples are: sex, alcohol, drugs, loose living, doing your thing is alright, and what ever makes you feel good. None of these teachings is the correct way of telling the student the complete truth, we all have a stake in how you live, and how it is going to affect others. Our thing in life might have an influence on some one else. They see you drinking alcohol in public, they think that it is alright for them to do the same, some smoke or use drugs in public, then they think that this is alright, go and use as many women as you possible can, they say do what you will as long as it makes you feel good. These teachings make it easier to not consider your fellow man in your decision. You make it all about you and what ever is good for you and make you feel good, regardless of how others is affected by this selfish decision. I believe that there are many things in our society that should be changed, but doing your own thing is not one of them. Perhaps if you were on an island all unto yourself, then you would not be affecting others, maybe then you would be able to do your own things. We are in a close society that reflects everything you do, everything you say and your life style in general will affect other people. Our influence over those who is astride the fence, not knowing which way to jump off, is greatly in doubt in which way they should jump. These people can be easily persuaded to jump off in the wrong direction of life. This is not always a good teaching, doing your own thing, for as long as it makes you feel good. We have a responsibility unto others to tell the truth and to show to the best of our abilities to others who are astride the fence in which direction they should jump off. This is one man's opinion.

My opinions are formed and became decisive, after working with, working around, talking to people that were in these situations. Opinions are from seeing these needs in people's lives. Some have told me of the reasons for them wanting to give up on life. They have said that no one cared for them, so why should they care for anyone else. They adopted the philosophy of do what right for them and makes them feel good, forget about anyone else, how they feel and what they say, they have adopted this attitude because of teachings in part, and developing a hard no caring mentality toward any one else. This is where part of our greed and our dog eat dog mentality come from. Grab everything you can grab and do unto others before they can do it unto you. This is the wrong direction to look for a more positive answer to our many questions about this thing called life and its many ups and downs. We knew a couple that lived not too far from us, when used to live on N. Kirby the parents used to ask my wife to baby sit for them. The young boy was about ten years old. His parents could not get along as husband and wife; the man left the mother and moved to Los Angels, California. She remained in Portland, Oregon. The mother needed a baby sitter while she worked at her job. My wife was asked to do the baby sitting, she accepted and took on the job, and she had four children of her own and had to see after them and their well being. The mother, passed away a few weeks after she had my wife to baby sit for her. Thomas Horseman was the name of the young boy. The one son of my own and the young boy had made good friends. Thomas said his mother had passed away, due to the over- dose of sleeping pills. According to Thomas, his mother was lying in bed and could not go to sleep, she called for him to bring her the sleeping pills, in which he did as he was told to do, and she then took more than what was prescribed for her to take. She went to sleep and never regained consciousness. Medical personnel arrived and found her to be deceased. The State soon took over the case and asked my wife if she would take up the responsibility of seeing after him. My wife accepted after some serious thoughts. Thomas was glad to be part of our family. He looked upon my wife as his mother and gave her all the respect that a child of her own would give her. Thomas looked upon me as being a father for him, something that he never had.

Thomas loved mother and all rest of our families. My family and my wife's family were loved. This was the only people that he knew. Mother and father would become his grand parents, same as our children; Thomas had someone that he could feel part off, some where that he could call home. Thomas, was a bright young boy, he had many talents. He was and still is, a good artist and printer, he also like poetry and write poems. Thomas lived with us for six or seven years before moving in with another family. Thomas has a sister and his father took her with him to California. Thomas never heard from his father or his sister for many years. His father became ill and was expected to pass on. Thomas never went to visit him while he was on his death bed. There were reasons for him not wanting to see him and he never wanted to discuss his father. It could have been too hurtful to talk about him. He could have seen things between his parents that he just as soon tries to forget. Some family adopted his sister that lived in California. He only received one letter from her since their father had passed away. It is my belief, that Thomas still harbors something deep down into his sub-conscious mind and maybe his heart.

Thomas, always keep in contact with us, he still thinks of us as being his family. We are the closest to what he had hoped a family would be about. I often took him and my son to fishing and camping with us. This is a life that he never knew. He had cousins, uncles, aunts, sisters and grand parents to try to make his life complete. Although Thomas has since married and has children of his own, he still is our family. He need some one that he can talk to, and to steer him in the right way. We try to guide him even unto this day, Thomas, insists that mother was and still is the one that taught him the Bible and the right way to live his life. He can recite many chapters and versus in the Bible. He is a constant reader of the Holy Bible. Perhaps mother never knew exactly, what kind of an effect that she had on Thomas life.

Many people that have tried to live the life that they talked about, probably will never know the seeds that they have planted, their reward is not forgotten. It is very important that we try to live a good life on this earth so others can say nothing bad about you. Whether they comment on your life style or not there is nothing negative that they can say about you when you passes on. You would have planted a seed for others to see and admire. We all have had short comings in one way or another, but this is human nature to make mistakes in life. The remedy for mistakes is to pray and ask for forgiveness for those things and try hard not to repeat the same mistake again, although, there will be other mistakes that we will make, or sometime intentionally commit sin. Either way, we have to be forgiven for our mistakes and sin. We cannot enter into Heaven with out being forgiven for our sins. Some time we are not aware that we have sinned; this is no excuse for us to enter into Heaven, without our sins being forgiven. We can know whether we are going to Heaven or not. We know the life that we have lived and we know if we have prayed for forgiveness for our sins and have turned our life around, in a way that is acceptable to God. We have to pray daily, asking for forgiveness for all things that we omitted to do or ask for forgiveness for things that we should have done that is pleasing in His sight. There are many things that we are commanded to do. There are things that we are commanded not to do. If any of the rules and commandments is not adhered to, then we have sinned. Many people give up on trying living a sinless life. They say the road is too narrow, there are too many restrictions, and they say they don't like to live this way. These people that say this, is the ones that don't won't to change their life style. The truth is, you can pay God now, or pay him later, at that time it might be too late to make a change. These are some of the requirements of us to get into Heaven. We have the scenario, which no one wants to die, but everyone wants to go to

Heaven. Some of us want to continue in our present life style, and still make it into God's Kingdom. We serve him and do what he asks of us, his mercy will bring us through. In the end of this life, we all will be judged on the opportunity that we have had on earth to prepare ourselves for that particular time. We have run a good race. His mercy and his love will bring us through.

The world's system is corrupt: if we had a perfect world to live in, then Jesus would not have a reason to come back down on earth to set up a perfect Government. He knew man would have a corrupt, un-just system here on earth and would not stand the ages of time. When he left this earth, he promised that he would come again. This time all the corruption, greed, injustices, lies, deception, robbers, thieves and all other sins will be done away with. First, everything that man ever had anything to do with will be consumed in fire. All sins, all of our materials that we use to build our earthly empire will be done away with. There will become a new Heaven and a new Earth. Saints of God will rule over the earth. His Holy angels will occupy this planet." Lucifer, and his entire host will burn in hell, all that follow the ways of Lucifer and his influences will join him there also". This is the word of the Holy Bible. It has been said and now it must come to the fulfillment of his Holy word. The governments of this world will be judged for allowing immorality and other corruption to infiltrate our intended way of living. We have done our own things and our own things have brought us to this point in human life. Our system of government has begun to crumble, planet is contaminated, food that we eat is filled with contamination, and greed has become the order of the day. Laws are made to legalize murder. Our selection of a presidential candidate is to allow smear, lies, exaggerated truths and nearly anything else to become elected to public office. I believe that there should be laws to regulate what is to be said, and limits on how far they will go in trying to deceive the public. The candidate should be well vetted before they are able to run for public office. These are the people that will be out front in the eyes off the public and they should be fined or eliminated from the running if they break the rules and laws that would govern their candidacy. These are the ones that should be above all the things that are not improving our way of looking to our leaders. When the public see and hear these things occurring on public television and on radio. This will give the impression of what our government is all about. There is a higher standard of doing things if we want to be a good representative of the people. They should be judged on their credibility, tell it like it is at the time. This is teaching the public that it is alright to use these tactics. The way you win is of the importance.

It seems if though the public approves of these smearing tactics. Some think this is the only way to get your point across to the people you want to represent. A change needs to be implemented to show a more positive side of our government. They are the ones who are supposed to show the rest of the citizens how to live. Win on their ability, and win on the truth. Show a positive candidacy, lies, exaggeration, deceit and anything goes is a negative, and selfish way of winning anything, this is one man's opinion, many will agree and there will be many who will not agree. If we want others to think and do the things that are right before the people that you want to represent, then a change is necessary to gain respect for our leaders. More respect would be given to our elected officers in public positions; if they would exercise the correct leadership instead of saying the correct words in trying to win over the votes of the citizens they will say mostly anything to garnish their vote. Deception seems to be the order of the day with these people seeking public office. Did we, the citizens, create this type of environment, or do we just like to see and hear smear tactics? It does anyone any good in trying to establish the public trust in the officers.

This game has been played for centuries, the best lie, and the one that can deliver the most smear, seems to be the one that garnishes the votes. The public should expect a different type of a public candidate who seeks the top job in our society and in the world. In achieving to become a candidate to fill the highest position in this nation, more should be expected of them on their character, too much smearing and too much deception in our politics. In this election of a President, I have seen too much of the wrong things invoked into the campaign.

Inciting hate and degrading of the opposition, trying to stir- up the pot. Focusing in on those who would hate on racial or any other grounds, hopefully, a change in the way we do business will end. We are yet to show the very best that we can to the rest of the world. We first must clean up our own house, then perhaps, we can teach other nations about our just and democratic system.

This is one man's opinion, you may or may not agree, but this is the way that I have seen the system work. I came to my opinion through reading, looking at and listening to the candidates for office. There would be some that would try to turn back the progress that have been made by dedicated, sincere hard working people that seek a better tomorrow. Some want to roll back the hands of time, the way of their ancestors, the sins of their fathers and their mothers. Progress will continue, and there will be a few pit falls here and there, but the power that guides us is more powerful than the power of the opposition. God raises people up to carried on his will. Each of those trail blazers of the past had to fulfill their mission that they had been given. These dedicated and obedient trail blazers had a job in blazing the trail only so far, then another blazer would rise up to continue blazing the trail. As each person or group of people heeded to the call and carried out their mission, the way is being made clearer. Still we have much to clear out of our way. We can see the journey ahead of us. God has a plan and no man can stop what He has intended to do. Those who want to be part of this trail blazing team need only a change of heart and a new out look for the future of this nation and of our world. I believe through the sins of our fathers that we have a debt to pay; this debt is owed to God. There will be the Biblical rule in play and it will be enforced by God. This rule is reaping and sowing. There is no doubt that we have sown some bad seeds, therefore, we will reap the results of our seeds that we have sown. We as a people or as an individual will not escape what have been spoken off. These reaping of seeds can be acquired through our human seeds two, three or even more generations in the future. This is the law of the harvest. Reap what you sow, we might as well expect the unexpected, things are going to happen on an even larger scale. We refuse to acknowledge our short comings, and some seem to want to continue on the same old losing course.

Traveling this journey of life, I met another Black man that had been traveling in the same direction that I was traveling. His name is Joe Hawkins, him and I had the same destination in mind, he had recently came up from Los Angeles, California." He told me about his life in the big city and why he had to escape from there." He was born and went to school there. He came from a Christian home and his parents were together until their deaths. Before they had passed away, their greatest concerns were: the well fare of his sisters and his brothers, and to trust in God always. Joe became a wayward child, he wanted to do his own thing, drinking, staying out late at night, running with friends and getting into trouble. His practices continued for a few years, and then he realized that his life had to be changed, it was a slow process in making this change, but he knew God, he had prayed for forgiveness for his past wayward life style for God to help him to become a different person. God answered his prayers and told him to leave this City, and to come up to Portland, Oregon. He obeyed and came to Portland to start his new life. It was not easy for him when he first came to Portland, but obedience and determination got him through the difficult times. He had no place to sleep and no place to eat, he eventually, was let into the Salvation Army's shelter home until he could get his feet under him. He found a job and eventually moved into an apartment. He did not have any people in Portland and did not know anyone out side of the shelter. There he met people that had similar problems as his own. When he began to let Christ come into his heart, his life and his complete out look on life changed for him. Joe progressed in Portland and became a dedicated Christian and laborer in the Church. This is where Joe, has been ever since he decided to let God guide his life. Today, we are the best of friends, we occasionally; go places together and thank God for the distance that we have traveled through life. Joe met a young woman and they became interested in each other and eventually, they got married, he is a happy man until this day. His joy and his praise all go to God. Joe knew only God could make this all happen. This was a good account of his life. The life that he now lives and all the beneficial experiences that he had acquired in growing up.

From being out into the wildness of life, there is something about a person that love God, there is a way that you will meet a person that loves the Christian walk; our meeting each other was incidental, two people traveling in the same direction and trying to reach the same destination. He has been a good friend. In my journey, I knew that I wanted to do something positive for other people that were struggling for a new direction in life. I occupied myself working in the house of the Lord. I joined the Usher board at the Church where I still attend. This was a good job to have in the Church. Everyone is so friendly, visitors come and are received with a warm welcome assisting people to good seating.

For me there is nothing like being in the house of the Lord, the people are so different there than the people that do not know the Lord, the warm smiles, the concerns for their brother's well being, this make a home for those who don't know which way to go and what to do with their lives, these people that's searching for peace and a place to belong. Being in church you can feel the warmth and affection that you receive from other worshipers. For those that truly love God, this is one big caring family. Serving on the usher board, we have different events through out the year, we have a dinner some time during the year, visit other churches; assist other churches with their functions when requested. I have worked with students in some schools as a mentor, trying to motivate the students that are slow and un-motivated students. I talk with the student to try to find what he or she is interested in. I wanted them to talk and tell me how they felt about certain issues in their lives. Much was learned about these slow students. Many had come from a one parent home, the mother usually, is the one that is left in trying to raise the family. The mothers are trying to work and put food on their tables; retain a place for them to sleep and purchase clothing for them. The mother's time is consumed with these chores. She can only spend a minimum amount of time with her family. Some students feel rejected; they feel like they are not being given attention to. The student adopts a negative mentality toward life and to people that come in contact with them. Many times these mental attitudes can be changed to a more positive way of thinking, through love and caring for the student; this can make a huge difference in one's life. There are many that have been receptive of this approach. All they want to know is that they are being loved and noticed. The one parent family should be commended for their many duties. The mother especially, should be commended for just being a mother. When there is no man in the house to put food on the table and no stable housing, the mother is playing a duel role in trying to provide for her family. Father is missing for many reasons. Some are in jail or prison, others just wanted out of his responsibility of being a bread winner. There are many reasons for the father being absent in the home. His children should receive the basic support from the father. I have observed the young married couples and their out look on marriage. Many don't take the time to try to make a go out of their marriages, when problems arise in the marriage, they think about divorce. They seem not to want to give and receive; each one thinks that he or she is right in the decision that is made. The pressure of marriage is too much for some to cope with. They think that they would be better off if they left the spouse. If there are children involved, they don't think of what the decision would do to them. This is a selfish way of trying to solve marital problems. Communication with one another and discussing their problems with one another is a beginning of a solution to their problem. My observation, either wants to give in to the other. Each person should be given the opportunity to address one's concern, one listen while the other talks. Each person should be able to state their concern. Many like to live as married couples, but without the responsibilities that go with it. They think that it is easier to pick up their belongings and just leave one another, without any obligation to the other. They have children without any of the responsibilities off a husband or wife. This is what our world has come to, a generation of children with only one parent being responsible. This is a cop-out of our man or woman hood. Most of our ancestors had it much tougher than we can imagine, but most found a way to bring them through the hard times. Most didn't have much, but they remained together and raised their families. God will punish those who do not exercise their duties as a mother or a father. The children are brought into this world, without them having any decision to do so. Before parents think about leaving one another, they should take a hard look at the consequences of what they want to do. Making sure that they are ready for parenthood, and will do what is necessary to raise the children in a normal setting. Children love to talk about their parents in a more positive setting.

Chapter Ten

Each child that is brought into this world should have more going for them than the previous generation. It is up to the parents to make sure that their children have a better chance at life than they had. Our society helps those of us that are having trouble in sending our children to school, scholar ships are offered to students that have promise. Some of these students receive academic and athletics scholar ships to some of the most prestigious schools in our society. There are some schools that will help a student to get employment after school hours. Parents should encourage their children to take advantage of these opportunities. This is a plus for our children and our society. The future of our country and our world will depend upon how well trained children of the future will be. Technology is in, the old way of working and getting the jobs done is on its way out. Only the most educated, the most motivated will receive the high paying jobs. During my youth, there were many that had the athletic skills to be a professional athlete in any of the major sports. Then the opportunity was not there. Today is a different story, apply yourself and the opportunity is there for you. Academically, there are more opportunities each year for motivated students, those that have a high degree of intelligence. If the student of today fails to take advantage of these opportunities, then the students from other nations will come and fill the void, and the local students will fall farther behind the rest of the world's students. It is a necessity for all of the young people to receive a good, reliable education, something that they can depend upon for life. When I attended and finished high school, you could be assured of getting a decent job. Now you will have to go far beyond just a high school education to be a success in life. High paying jobs is for the ones that have the best educational skills. It has become highly competitive for the students of today.

In America, I see a new race of people that is beginning to surface. In the future there will be fewer all whites and fewer all blacks in the hemisphere. The races will become a brown race; they will merge into one race of people. The culture will be a mixture of all races of people. There will be Native Americans, Hispanic, Asians, Africans, Far Easterner, and many other groups and tribes. This will form a one racially mixed society. There will be few full blooded groups left in America. In the future, there will be no one in America that could say that they are of one race or group, we all will have a mixture of many races and back grounds. I know this is what people had opposed from centuries ago here in the United States, although, the trend was started centuries ago. Slaves were the most common ones used to create this new race of people. The masters over the slaves had access to slave women to do with what they pleased; there were nothing that the male slaves could do about it. The new race had begun when the slave woman brought forth a child. The child was of mixed racial blood, many times the master tried to hide this child from the other slave masters and friends. Most of this was done without the knowledge of a spouse. Many Black male slaves that were made to breed with a white woman by the woman herself, she would call" rape" if the slave refused to do what she wanted him to do. Slaves were then taken out and hung, shot, even burned to death because of these lies. A white male did not have to pay for his wrong doing; he only had to keep the baby out of sight of his friends. Few had the courage of admitting his guilt. Europeans had started this mixing of the races when they first came to America, it started with the Native Americans. They were quick to mix with a woman of another race but un-willing for a male of any other race to mix with a white woman of their race, these selfish attitudes exists even until this day. Laws have been changed and mixed marriages are on the rise, but the mentality still exists today among those who want a one way mixing of the races. These mixtures of races will be the future leaders of our country. As children are born to these couples, even less attention is being paid to your racial back ground. There will be no one that could boast of their one blooded heritage. We will all be in the blood line. Perhaps this is the way that it was meant to be, we all becoming one in the last days upon this earth. There will be no one that try to insult you without insulting themselves, what ever he say you are, he is also the same thing, for they both come from the same blood line. These are the people of the future. Brown will be the color. Whites and blacks, Asian and Middle Eastern, all will have come together in the distant future.

My friend faces tragedy; Jack is the first person that I made friend with, in coming to Portland. We have done many things together. We attended high school together and we were in the National Guards together. Now he has been diagnosed with an eye disease. The things that he sees is very blurry and he see shadows of most objects. This is a tremendous back set for him and his family. Jack has always been a very spry and energetic person. He would always be ready to go and enjoy his life and enjoy others. He is going to have an operation for his sight in the near future. His wife said that he "feels down and he never go any place less she drives him there. I hope the operation to his eyes will come back to him. His wife is re-tired from her job of thirty-five years, so she is home with him all of the time. Times before, I had invited him out so we could talk about some of the good times that we had together. He refused most of the time. He feels if though his worth is no longer needed. I tried to re-assure him, he still had friends and they all pray for his recovery. Jack is like a brother to me and other friends. Those of us, who still have good health, should be thankful each day that we are alive, and that we can still do most of the things that we are accustomed to doing without any restrictions. It could happen to anyone of us at any given time. His beautiful wife, attend the same Church that I attend. One Sunday at Church services, "she asked me if I would talk to" Jack to try to persuade him to go out with me sometime. He needs to be out of the house and regain his confidence". That same Sunday after service, I told her that I would" stop by her house to chat with him for a while". During our chat, I asked him to attend one of our meetings that occur once a month, he said that he would consider it. I explained to him that he was under no obligation to join the club. The club members are made up of re-tire and most of them he knows. He wanted to know our club's mission and our operational procedures? He also wanted him and I to wanted go out to lunch one day. I accepted and told him that his time was my time, looking forward to us having a day out.

We have seen and heard of many of our friends that had either passed on, or went to jail or prison fortunately, neither one of us have ever been in jail or arrested for any crime. We were sorrow to hear about those that had passed on. Those that went to prison of jail had a choice, they became involved with the wrong people or they had done something criminal. Those that survive prison life, and come out into society say that they had seen the light. The light was always there for them, but they refused to see it. They chose the easier way out, stealing, robbing, burglary, drugs and other criminal activities. They chose the fast lane. This truly was a road to no where. Now most have trouble getting a good job. Many resort back to a life of crime and end up back in prison or jail. These people have gone through their lives and accomplished nothing. Some had children out of wed lock. The children would be without a father around to keep them in line. The children go to school with a chip on their shoulders be denied the things that other children receives love and someone that cares for them. These men did not consider what they were doing to their children's lives. These are the children that will become un-motivated. They will think that no one cares or loves them. This is my club's mission; try to redirect the young people's thoughts, giving them something that is more positive. If we can change a few from this mentality, and put a more positive out look on life for these children, then I believe that we would have made a difference in some of the children's life, we also know that it is hard for a one parent to give the children everything that they needs. This is especially true when there are more than one or two children in the family. We have seen cases where the parent themselves, have all but given up on life. Their life seems to have gone down the drain. They adopt the negative attitude; they think the world had passed them by. When the one parent stop trying to make a better life for the family, then the family will become a dependant of the State, losing the parent right to raise and govern her family as they wanted. After telling my friend Jack, of all these consequences of the children, he approved of what we were trying to do.

Billy Ray Bridges, another high school friend and first cousin to Jack. We had a friendly relation ship, and so did many more high school students. Billy Ray, received the nick name of "goat", his first cousin Jack had given him that name, reason for calling him that was never known to me, however, he would respond to that nick "name" and did not think it was derogatory or insulting to him. During that time, all the young people were referred to something other than their given name. When these other names were call out, we knew who they had referred to. Billy is one of the cousins that joined the National Guard with me. He later was drafted into the active Army for missing too many drills. Billy had to spend three years in the active Army for absenteeism. This extra time away from his home and his friends made a better man out of him. Billy was a nice person to talk to, but he did not like to be told what he should do. When he came back from the army, he was a completely different person, he was more mature and you could have a decent conversation with him. He became a listener rather than a talker, Billy had met a young lady that he later married and had two children. He had been hired in a good paying job and supported his family. Many years had passed before I saw Billy again. He told me that he had acquired diabetes and took his treatment at the University Medical School in Portland. We were glad to see one another, we talked about old times. He seems to take the disease with ease, he did not seem to be worried about his condition, in many ways and he was the Billy that I knew in our school days. Many years had passed before I would hear of him again. Jack's wife told me that "Billy had suffered a stroke" and the stroke had left him in a bad way. He could barely walk and murmur his words". This was truly a bad thing to hear. She said that he was in good spirit, regardless of his condition his daughter sees after him. His wife had died a few years earlier, and he moved in with his daughter. We pray for his recovery.

Donald Burns; this was another good friend of ours. We were raised and grew up in the same neighborhood. We went to the same high school. Donald was a working man all through high school. When he had week ends off, he would attend parties that were given by someone that we had gone to school with. He was a close friend to Jack. It seem if though they had much in common, but he eventually enlisted into the Army, and when he had served his time there and came back home to Portland, Oregon to live for a few years and his next move would be to Alaska, a place far away from where he was born, there he was assured good Government Job with the United States Government, he started his own business in the news paper industry and he was successful in that business. Donald, found a young lady in Alaska that was from Portland also, they became friends and they later married. He remained in Alaska, and made his home there. He would occasionally return back to Portland to visit his parents and friends. The Alaskan weather and surroundings seem to agree with his well being. Donald was missed by his friends and his family since he moved to Alaska. This was the new frontier; there were un-limited opportunities for people that wanted a better life for themselves and their families. People came from all over the Country to take advantage of the opportunities there. Many were from the southern portion of the Country, from the eastern and the western sections of the Country. "He said this was an ideal place to work, play and to hunt and fish". Their days were different than in the lower States. During the snow season, most things came to a slow pace and most activities were confined to indoors. To drive the newly renovated high way, is a beautiful drive. Ice covered mountains, icy rivers and lakes, snow covered mountain peaks. Grizzly bears, moose and other wild life that is the native animals of this frozen territory. The Eskimos that have live there for many centuries carry on life in their culture as they have for hundreds of years. My sister and her husband took a cruise by ship to this beautiful, icy paradise. "They said the trip was once in a life-time experience. The travel by ship gave them the opportunity to see the huge glaciers and ice bergs, the deep stormy seas, whales and sea birds of all species". This is paradise. People, things, experiences, and my personal thoughts about my travel on this journey, are all factual.

People that I have talked with and their experience in some events may be interjected into my journey.

My thoughts on corruption in our Government denial of events that is part of our Country's history, mental adjustments and opportunities Close calls with death, hunting and fishing experiences in Mississippi, both on the farm and in the city, moving to Portland, Oregon, high schools that I attended, jobs that I held while starting a new life, my mate for life, my Army experience. There are other things that are mention in my biography of the long journey. I have always had an urge to put in writing the things that were stored within me. I wanted to express my feelings, observation and my encounter with some of the pit falls of life. When I was a young child growing up, the urge was there but did not have all the experience that I acquired as I became older. I have tried to give a complete trace of my life as I knew it from an early age. It would be impossible to give a day by day recording of my life, but all the important and major events that took place in my life is accounted for. Several reasons for me to write my journey: One of the reasons is that I had an urge to write something about my life, and the people that were instrumental in shaping my life. The other reason for wanting to write is for my children to have something that they could look back on in their lives, and to know more about their father and their grandparents, my sister and brothers, my cousins, uncles, aunts and some of the friends that I had in growing up. This will give them a little better understanding of how life was along the long journey.

Friends that I made along the way will never be forgotten, from the hot farms in Wesson, to Jackson and from Jackson to Portland, Oregon. I left good friends in one place and made good friends in another. The way that I feel toward these friends will never cease. I will always think of them when just sitting around thinking. We had to be united in Mississippi we all had to help one another. We had to survive and it took all of us sticking together to do that, no one had very much, but the people shared what they had with one another. The difference now is, we have become a people of independence and less helping one another. I have seen people that make a decent life for themselves, but forget to lend a hand to bring the ones that have less, up to a higher standard of living. For those that are less fortunate and is trying to make a go of life, we that have much should try to bring them up to a higher standard of living. There are combinations of things that keep some of the people down. Lack of education is one and probably, the most important, racial prejudices are another Motivation, living within the means of what you have. I have seen many of us that rather purchase a new car than try to purchase a home. Some like to dress too extravagant. We purchase things that are not a priority to us making a decent life and having a decent place to live and raise a family. Not excusing racism, education, criminal back ground and injustices, but there are things that we can do to make a better life for ourselves and family. Statements in this long journey are not meant to be negative, but if the truth is to be told, it will hurt or offend some of us. This is my thoughts, my observations, and my experiences. There will be some that will disagree with what is said through observations and opinions, but you cannot disagree with the on hand experiences that I have had. Although only two localities are spoken off in this journal, these practices are by no means limited to these locations. Reading papers, books, television news and other media information, the situation is basically the same, even worse in some areas of our country. I believe that we still are one of the best countries in the world to live in. When I see poverty with no end and children is blessed to receive only one meal per day, that is if they can, then we still have much to be thankful for. It is true; we could be a much better country. There are problems that we as a country should focus on and try to eliminate. The forces of evil are strong and it will take a strong will of all the people to eradicate the prejudices and the injustices that keeping our country from going forward and progressing. I cannot understand some of our seniors, professing to be Children of God and good Christians, but still act and do the opposite of what God is all about. You make the comparison, you be the judge and see how we measure up to what is needed. They have sinned. But there can be forgiveness for sin if you are willing to admit the sin and stop doing that, which is wrong, but to deny and continue to live in sin, and then this is a gross mistake. It seems to be proud that send a person into denial of certain problems, sooner that you face reality and try to correct it, the better it will make you feel and God will be pleased.

History is made daily; each person that travels through this life has a story to tell about the events that took place in their lives. We each have taken different roads to reach the same destination. Some had a wonderful life in traveling this journey; others have experienced hard ships and disappointments in their travel. Sights are set for the same destination. There will be some that will not reach the other side of life. They will falter along the way; they will give up on trying reaching the promised destination. The only way that they can be assured of getting there, is to keep their sights forward, knowing where they are trying to get to. Making this journey will take some assistance; we will have to carry a route map. The map tells us what route to take and the tools that we will need to get there. The Holy Bible and the Spirit of God will be the only tool that we will need to have a successful trip. We will not be able to make this trip alone; we will need help in every foot of the way. The obstacles have been placed in our way and they are too large for us alone to remove them." Lucifer, the mighty one has placed these obstacles in our path, hoping that we will detour off the right pass. God, the almighty will remove those obstacles that are in our way. There is no way we can have a successful trip traveling this journey alone. Spiritual guidance is what we need on our travel. Many things will get in our way and try to derail us but to be steadfast and rely upon the tools that you have been given to make this journey. This life's journey is too much for one to do it alone. We only have to ask for his assistance, he is always ready to assist those who call upon him for the hard and difficult things that belie in our pass way. The journey was never promise to us of being an easy journey; he did promise that we would make the journey if we relied upon him, using the tools that he has given to us. He never meant for us to travel alone, he has always been there for us. We only need to ask for his help. He never forces himself upon anyone, but he is there for us when called upon to help us get through to the other side of life. This is his promise.

We all are different; we came into this world with a certain difference, from our genetics to our thought processes. However, he gave each person a certain amount of goodness from birth; we have a head start on the evil things that we would face in this life. We know from day one that there are certain things that are wrong. At an early age, we might not know what it is that show us that it is wrong to do certain things and to say things that is not the correct way of doing it, but that built in spirit will make you feel something is wrong, it just don't seem to be the right way of thinking or doing things. This head start is the goodness that was instilled in us as humans from our creation. We only need to be taught and exercise the goodness that has been placed in us. Even in our later years in life, it is even more apparent. There is a small something that is within us to let us know that something that we have done or something that we were thinking was not of the right spirit. This is where we should seek to find the correct spirit, and to do what the correct spirit tells us to do or to say. There is only one way to chose. You will either follow the evil spirit, or you will follow the good spirit. This is where we need to seek the teachings of the Bible and let the Spirit of the Lord guide us. Guide us in decision making, in our thoughts, and in our deeds. Although goodness is placed within each of us from birth, we need to grow and materialize this kindness and goodness that is placed into each human being. Failure to exercise the goodness that is placed within us will allow the evil things to creep in to our thought process and cause bad things to happen. We all was created to bring pleasure to God, we cannot bring pleasure to him, when we are not exercising his will. Reading and being taught his will, is the way to know his will. This will always be something that is positive. It may be to help your self or to help someone else. Sometimes God might use evil to correct something that needs correction. He works in many ways, we cannot say how he will work situations out, but every time he does is for the advancement of man kind. His ways are different than our ways. He is God and his ways from our ways are as different, as the day is from the night or His Heaven is from the earth. We know the way for us to follow is plain. We don't know the ways of Him. We should never try to figure out in what way that he will act to situations. He assured us that he would act. You cannot talk bold about the Spirit of God, unless you have been touch and seen his Spirit work. Personally, I do not have any doubt of his love and almighty power; I see it on a daily basis.

Words of wisdom; this is what I would say to any one wanting to change their life style or wanting to do more in their relation with the Almighty, if you are seeking the kindness and love of Jesus Christ, and want to know more about him, seek him in all the ways that you can. Attend Church, ask other members of the Church about your concerns, read the Holy Bible, pray for guidance and understanding of his word, consult Pastors or other people that is responsible for bringing new converts to Christ." These people have been placed in these positions for our needs. These are the ones that have knowledge and have been placed there by the Spirit of God. For those who want to go farther in their Christian walk is to keep going forward, asking God what He will have you to do. In what position in this walk would he have you to pursue. Nothing will stop you from doing what God would have you to do. Tell others about his love for us all, and there is a better way in this life than what the world can offer unto us. This is the only thing that we can carry on to the other side of this life with us, our obedience, love, and our deeds that we have exercised on this earth while we were alive. There is nothing else that is material in this life that we can take with us to the other side. "What profits a man to gain the world and lose his soul" this is Biblical. Gain all you want, make as much money as you can, own as much property as you can, but in the end of time for you on earth, there is nothing that you can take with you to the other side. The only thing that will stand the ends of time is what you did for Christ while he gave you time on earth. We should try as hard as we can to love everyone. This is probably the hardest of all the commandments, yet it is a requirement from God. He said," How can you love him in whom you have never seen, and yet hate your brother in which we see daily". It is hard to love someone that despitefully uses you and hate you and someone that constantly do evil unto you, those that will intentionally, do you harm for no reason other than hate. This is perhaps the hardest of all the Commandments. This is what we are to do.

If we can keep this Commandment, I believe the rest of them will be much easier for us to conform to. Many people have died because of hate, many have been denied the due process of law, and many have been denied many things because of hate. Wars have been started and many lives lost because of some one preaching and teaching hate. All the other Commandments involve love, this truly the hardest in my view, of all the other commandments. We still have to obey the others, but love for the rest of them will come, if you first love your fellow man, then we can truthfully, say that we love God. He requires this of each human being. Obeying his Commandments is not an option, we cannot pick and choose who we will like and who we will hate. It is my belief, that there are satanic reasons for us to hate and not love. When we hate there are consequences that we have to bear. Hate can lead to the ill being of an individual. Hate eats away at your inside, ulcers occur, cancer may occur, heart disease, may develop and many more sickness that may take place in our body. Our spiritual aspirations may come to an end or impede our spiritual walk." There is no quitting making this walk, you either serve God or you will serve Lucifer", you cannot have it both ways. You will love one and hate the other, or you will hate one and love the other. God said that he was a jealous God, and we should not have any other god or gods before him. Our love is the most important thing that we can offer to our fellow human beings. We cannot do this until we love what God has laid before us. We will love him and do what he asks of us to do in life. We all need God's help in trying to obey his Commandments, he gave us the tools to work with when read and obey his words. When we have trouble in trying to carry out His commandments, He wants us to ask him for help and guidance along the way. If we try it alone, we are doom for failure. We need his assistance to help us along in this walk toward perfection. Always working toward this goal, this is the only way that we can be accepted into his Kingdom. He said that it is not his will that any man should perish. He is always ready and able to assist us in our life's struggle toward a life of perfection. I speak of these things because I have gone through the love and hate scenario, hate is a no win situation for us.

The Long Journey

    This is the final chapter to my biography; this is written for and about all of the loved ones in my journey, in recognition of all of my friends that I left behind in Mississippi, all of my relatives and my dear grandparents, my dear sister and two brothers, my uncles and aunts, cousins. Last but the most important in my life, my dear mother and father who stayed together and saw their dream come true. This is also recognition of all of the new friends that I made when I first move to Portland. These people will never be forgotten as long as I am alive. These people stuck by me always, during the worst of times and during the best of times. They were always there for me if I needed their assistance. We now have a Black potential, Presidential candidate, I hope he makes it. The opposition is strong. There are many obstacles in his way; they have tried many things to try to derail him. There have been lies, racial insults, and any thing else that they could throw at him. He is qualified for the job and the only thing that will keep him out of the White house is his mix racial blood line. He is black/white. His mother White and his father was Black. This is the first time a Black person has ever gone this far in running for the Presidency. There have been records set in nearly all phases of the campaign. He had record turn outs for his speeches, he won the primaries, and he is on a good road to win the Presidency. The people are ready for a change in our Government. He has knowledgeable people that are around his campaign. There are more White people for him being elected for the Presidency than were expected and there have been those in the minority that try hard to derail him, Insults, lies smears, and anything else that they can throw in his pass. I believe that God have a plan for this young Black man. This is his time to take the baton and head toward the finish line. Only God could work in the hearts of these die hearted people to make them have a change of heart. This is the first none White candidate that have ever run for such an office. All of the ground work had been laid by the" trail blazers" that were before him.

    I hope to see a Black president in the white house in my life time. This would only be a joke to some of the older people. My parents never would have thought of a Black becoming to the presidency. They all had dreams of someday this would be possible. The thing is, they did not live long enough to witness it. This candidate is a perfect candidate to run for the position, he is half White and half Black, he is a little of both races. He can communicate with all people with different back grounds and racial make up. It is my belief, if he had been an all Black candidate, he wouldn't have gotten this far in the running. There is some lead way there by him being of both races. He has received good review from most of the voting public. Timing was everything, the right man at the right time, the economy, health care, jobs, wars, and the corruption that is in the white house. People have grown tired of all the high energy prices, food and other things essential to our survival. I believe this is the time that God will place a man of God in the white house to lead this country back to him. There are Christians that are praying for a change in our leadership, someone that will put Him first in decision making and look to him for guidance. In the Bible God did establish Governments, and He tore them down when they went their own way and forgot him. We all should pray for a man of God to fill this position of leading the greatest Country on earth. It is time for the rest of the world to see us practice what we have been teaching them. Be true Christians and not hypocrites. We have been telling other nations of the world one thing, and living another way. I believe that we as a nation have one last chance to make it right with God and to other nations of the world. If we fail to turn our nation around, then I believe that we will be taken over by the enemies of our way of life. One world government is already in the makings, life as we know it, is coming to a halt. The die hearts and the likes might as well face up to the evidence that is coming before us on a daily basis. These problems are not limited to the United States; this is a world's problem. Every nation has felt the squeeze. It is going to take a global unification to control the economy. We have allowed greed to take over. Some of the poor countries of the world have felt the squeeze for many decades. Now the squeeze is coming to the wealthiest countries in the world. The world is going through a major change, this cannot be denied. There will be many that will claim to have the answer for our problems but there is no real solution in sight. We have allowed this greed to fester for too long. This is the results. We in America knew what were going on many years before it got to this point in our economy. Greed has been in place in our society, festering on poor people for decades. We allowed this to happen and now people seem if though they are surprised that we are in the predicament that we find ourselves in this day. Those that have achieved their wealth from greed and deceit will not go down easily. They will spend billions of dollars to retain their wealth and the way they accumulated it. The rich never have enough wealth. They want more and more all of the time. They will starve, kill, misuse, abuse, and any thing else that they can get away with to get more and to hold on to what they have already accumulated and denied others from succeeding in life. Agree or disagree, this is one man's opinion to the ills of our nation and of our world. Politics is one thing that the people in power do not want to share with any poor people that seek political office in form. They are afraid that their age old tactics, and their ways of accumulating wealth will be found out, the secrecy of what really goes on in the political circles will be impeded upon. Most wealthy politicians are welcomed to the circle of corruption. They all have the same things in mind. The objective is to exercise power and control over the ones that are less fortunate and to keep them there. These politicians are the power hungry ones, the ones that dedicated to do these deeds at any cost. We even elect and appoint these people with these views toward the poor to keep them without a voice and without any power to make a decisive change in how business is carried out. We have one good thing that is in our favor, we have the power to elect who we think that will work for our needs and concerns. This is where we are ahead of some of the other nations of the world. The only thing is the money that it takes to run a fair and just campaign. Money is the driving force in elections.

Dreams of my mother; two years after my mother had passed away, I had a dream of her coming back for her love ones. She arrived aboard a passenger train that stopped in front of my home, she was in the engineer's cab of the train with two more people, and they seem to be the engineers of the train. There were many people aboard the passenger train and they were all waving their hands at me through the windows of the train with smiles on their faces. For some unknown reason, my family and I were waiting her arrival. I had taken a position in the living room, looking out of the picture window when the train pull up and stopped just right of the window on the street, mother jumped or flew out of the window in a split second, and she arrived at the front door of the house. I went to the front door to meet her and was glad to see her. I welcomed mother into the house and tried to make her sit and relax for a few minutes, a soft drink was offered to her to fill her thirst after a long ride. Mother refused, she asked me "if we were ready to go. She said that she would drink something after she reaches her destination" Her reason for her not wanting to have a drink of water or soft drink was that she did not know what we had in it. The house was full of family members, my sister and her family was there, my brother and his family, there were a few close friends of the family there also. When mother asked me if we were ready to go I immediately, went to the back rooms of the house to round up the rest of the family and friends, we did not want to leave anyone behind. My sister's husband was on the outside of my house sitting in the driver's seat of my motor home reading a book with his head being bowed downward. There were two small windows in our family's room that had a clear observation of the motor home which was parked close to the rear of the house where the family room is located. I knocked on the window to get his attention, to let him know that mother had arrived and she was ready to go. All the family was gathered and the dream ended. I told my family about the dream and there were many that tried to explain it. We all agreed that mother came back to gather her family. She was on the Heavenly train, and bound for Heaven. She came back for her love ones so we all could be together once again. This was a dream so realistic and clear, the long train that was filled with well wishers and having smiles on their faces. The engineers and mother all dressed in white, the speed that she left the train and was at the front door. All of the family having knowledge of her coming to get us. It has a spiritual significance. She wants us to be ready when the train comes to pick us up. This dream will be with me through out my life here on earth.

The Long Journey

My second dream of mother; this dream occurred a few years after the first dream of mother on the train In this dream, the family and a few friends were walking through a dense forest, there was a narrow pass that led through the dense forested area, the family was all together in close ranks. Suddenly, Mother had noticed a couple of the people that came with us were not with us any more, we continue to walk on this narrow path, hoping that they would catch up with us. We came to the end of the pass at one end of the forest and saw this huge shack or a house that was deep into the forest. This was our destination for the time being. We had a friend that was with us, his name was Green Baum, and he had been a fellow employee with me on my job at the transit system. We both had re-tired from fare inspection. He was with the rest of the family coming through the forest. When we arrived to the house and began to settle down, mother instructed me to go back and look for those that was no longer with us. My friend and I left the house in pursuit to find the two that were lost. As we both, walked down this long narrow pass way through the forest, we came upon a meadows at the end of the pass way. There we found five bodies lying flat on their backs with an army green tarp covered over their bodies; they were in a straight line, side by side. Their feet were exposed and their heads were covered. We did not know who these bodies were. I went one by one kicking the feet of each body to see if though we could get a response. There was no response to four of the bodies. They were dead. The fifth body was alive, but barely. When I kicked the foot of the fifth body, it rose up from the lying position to a sit-up position and exposed his chest and the terrific wound that he or she had suffered. Only the cavity portion of chest was exposed. We could not make out the face of the body. When the body rose up, this frightened us and we immediately, started to run back to the house that we had left from. I went back on the same path that we had taken to come out to that point. My friend Green Baum took another route. He was only a few yards from me traveling on a different pass, but headed in the same direction. I heard him talking to someone who had stopped him along the way back to the house. There were talking back and forth.

Chapter Eleven

This was the last time that I saw him. When I arrived back at the house, mother wanted to know if we had seen the two people that we had set out to find. I didn't want to tell mother and the rest of the family of what we had encountered. Father insisted that I tell the family of what we had encountered; mother did not want to know what I had seen out in the forest. Father insisted, so I did tell the family of what we had seen. We did not see the two people that we were looking for. There were five un-known bodies that were lying out there in the forest if though they had fallen in battle. The body that had a bad chest wound and the other four bodies seem to be placed there by someone for a pickup. That was a bad dream. My friend was never heard off again. After telling the family of the terrible ordeal, the dream ended. Many things happen to you when you are sleeping, some times revelation is shown to you on things to come or things that had been. Some dreams are just dreams. However, there is a lesson to be learned from most of them. Many times we have to just wait on the revelation of some dreams to see if and when it will come true. God spoke of young and old, having visions and dreaming dreams, so there is some merits too many of our dreams. There was another dream that I had that rested on my conscious. This was a dream of my wife. I didn't want to tell her about the dream, but something kept urging me to tell her. The dream was not a pleasant dream, so I hesitated to tell her of what I had dreamt. I tried to encourage her by telling her it was only a dream and it had little or no meaning at all. The dream started at a huge gathering, either in a foot ball stadium or a basket ball court. There were many spectators, and workers at the stadium. My wife had gotten lost in the crowd of people and we could not find her. The dream showed her with a weary look on her face, walking through the crowd with her head pointed straight ahead of her, she seem to be walking in a trance. A few of family and friends set out to find her and had no luck in doing so. We then talked to one of the security personal there and told him our story; he then immediately put out a search for her, and called her name on the microphone. She later was discovered, walking in a sea of humanity. The security notified us of their finding her. All of our hearts jumped with joy to see her again. Again, this was an un-explained dream. We did not know how to explain it. She had just wondered away from the rest of us. Maybe she got lost from us through the large crowd of people. It could have been intentional, or maybe it was just another dream without meaning.

A word of caution, do not over-look all of your dreams, some might have a significant meaning to you or someone that you love. We do know that the ones that do have meanings is the ones that we should take heed on. Sometime a dream is clear and precise, others seem to make no sense at all. Those that don't make any sense, you still should be aware and cautious. Dreams appear in many ways, it is hard to tell which ones are true or which ones is just a dream. My mother used to dream about many things. Most of them came true. However, she was a dedicated woman of God. She prayed constantly, and look to God for her every need and participation in certain things in our society. It was a dream that was shown to her about the home that she and her family would some day own, it was a dream that she had received in my brother's death, it was a dream that she had about me and my family purchasing the home that we live in. I could think of many things that were shown to her in dreams. We all took her dreams as fact. We have heard of her dreams and watched for many of them come to pass. She had a close walk and talk with the only one that she put complete faith in, when God revealed a certain thing in her dream that she should be concerned about, she would tell the family about it most of the time. We just waited until her dreams were full-filled. If you have a praying family, do not take their dreams too lightly. In conclusion of my journey, I ask prayer for our country. I would like to see people in our country to practice what we preach. Pray that we elect someone that love to do the right thing by all. Nations are watching us as we move toward our election cycle of who will lead us into the future. We need a God fearing leader, someone that will put him first in decision making. We need a leader who seeks peace.

We need a younger, more intelligent, more educated leader to work with other nation's leaders. War should be the last option for settling the world's problems, not the first. In the past, we have been too quick to exercise our military might first, and talk to solve a problem last. We need new leadership to carry us into the twenty first century. Someone with a vision, a leader that can understand the problems of other countries, understands their culture, their people and their land helping those who ask for our help in making progress. This will be the best way that we can exercise our concern for the world's problems. We set a good standard that the rest of the nations can see and bring democracy to their people. So far they have seen some of the worst in our society. We have not lived what we have preached to others. In many cases, we have lived more of a hypocritical life style than a Christian one. There are still many good Americans, some that want to be a credit to what we teach, some want the rest of the world to know that not all of us are hypocritical in what we say and do. The greed, murder, and deceit seem to shine brighter than the good that is done. We need to get rid of the old ways of doing things along with some of the old leaders that resist change, and replace them with people with a new vision. This is my personal thought, and my personal observations of our system of government. In writing this journey, I wanted to say exactly how I felt about situations in our country and in our world. This is only one person's opinion. Some things mention is my experiences, and experiences of my love ones. Other information is gathered through news media, books, and talking to some of the older citizens. This information combined with my experiences on my journey, helped me in writing the journey of my life. This truly was a challenge, trying to put into writing the information that I had stored within me. This was my life's long dream, which some day I would take the time and the patience to put into writing, my thoughts and my vision, and the reality of the world's condition. Each person has to tell their own life's journey. I am sure that we all have a story to tell about our lives, although some may be different than others, our destination is the same. We started from birth. We lived many years upon this earth, and then it is time for us to pass on. The only thing that we can carry with us is the credibility that we had while traveling this journey, a journey from birth to death. This is the passport to the other side of life. My hope is, that we have our passport in order while traveling this journey and trying to enter the other side of this life. The journey is long. It is full of distractions, objects will be in our way, but we should have the right tools to remove the obstacles and continue our journey to our hopeful destination.

In closing out my journey, there are things yet to be said. Credit should be given to all the citizens of our country in trying desperately to make this country and other nations of the world a better place for all of the world's citizens to live. We have not given these citizens enough credit in trying to advance others in the world. Americans of all walks of life are working on a daily basis to try to educate, teach, and preach and other ways of trying to make a better life for us all. In spite of all the negativity that has occurred in our past history, we are a symbol of democracy and change. It is the citizens that are using the Biblical principles to try to advance our people. They know what is needed to turn our world around to the right way of living. We know that there are some that working equally, to disrupt this way of doing these things. They benefit from deceit, corruption, murder, robbery, and any other thing that are a benefit to them. These people's cares less about others in the world, they only cares about their own greed and corruption, what ever it takes to advance their profits and power over other people of the world. The truth is that the quiet and few in our world, is working hard to keep things moving in a positive direction. There are some that is astride the fence, these are the ones that take life as it exists, not caring one way or another, excepting things in any form or condition. They seem to be satisfied with whatever goes on in the world and in our society. Being neutral will not get the change that is needed to advance our world. Doing nothing is an endorsement of corruption, murder, robbery, drugs, deceit and other things that would hinder the advancement of a more positive world and our nation. If you help the few that is for a better world and a better nation, then you are doing a positive contribution to the nation and advancement of the world and our nation. If you agree with the current situation in our world, then you have endorsed the very thing that is slowing our progress toward a better world and a better nation. It is my hope that we will all see the light and change courses. The journey is long and not yet completed. We need to continue our travel until our destination has been reached. This is my hope and my personal opinion.

    The biggest obstacle in our way, is greed, this is the main thing that contributes to all of the other negatives that we having to face on this journey. From greed, come corruption and from corruption come deceit, then robbery and eventually, murder. Greed has contributed to all of the ills that is in our world and in our society having greed, has caused people to go without the necessary things in life to survive the way that they should, the medicine that they need and a way to pay the high cost of getting it, decent shelter and a way to pay for it, food which is a very important element of survival. All of these things accumulated from greed. Those who have more than enough for their families to live a good life, is not satisfied with that, they seem to want all that they can get from any and all that they can get it from not caring about the ones that they are taking these things from, It seem that the rich never gets enough, the more that they take, the more that they want to take. This is the mentality that the wealthiest people in our world and in our nation have adopted. There will always be some poor people in the world just because of mentalities such as this. Whole nations have suffered under this kind of mentality. It all can be traced back to greed, the taking of the world's resources for personal gain and enrichments. Some of the nations and citizens of our society have been taken advantage off; lack of education is one of the main reasons. Not knowing what is taking place in their lives financially, they are being over charged in nearly ever thing that we purchase, from shelter to transportation, from the food that we need to the medicines that we need to survive, from the clothing on our backs to the education that we pursue. When it is all said and it is all done, greed is the front runner to the haves and not haves; however, we do know that there will be some of our citizens that will remain poor and always trying to measure up. There will be some that will not take the advantage of the opportunities that is before us. Some will still be unmotivated for one reason or another. It has been said that the poor will always be with us. This is a fact of life. The amount of poor could be reduced, if only some stop taking much more than what they should. My opinion is again based upon observations, reading, news media, conversations, and opinions.

Democracy: our democracy gives us the right to speak out on the things that we disagree with, and the laws uphold these rights. We can disagree with anything that we choose to disagree with, as long as there is not violence involved, and there is no inciting of insurrection or rioting. We should however be careful of what we say and how we say it. We should not use defamation to exercise our disagreement to issues or to someone else. These disagreements should be made without violence or defamation of someone's character. The right of every man to speak the truth and to speak what is in his heart to speak without being penalized for doing it. There are things that we should take into consideration when we are expressing ourselves. We should know if what we are expressing will bring hurt and discredit to the issues that you disagree with. Disagreements should be based upon some factual situations. A proven fact can be based upon something that you read from a book, experience, credible information, and other sources of information. We should not disagree with someone or something unless, we have a source of information in which we can argue the point. The one that is being disagreed to should respect the right of the one to disagree, this do not make him right, neither does it make you wrong, this is a mutual respect for one's opinion. In giving respect to one's opinion, you will receive respect in giving your respect. It is possible that both parties have a certain amount of truth in their disagreement, and it is possible that neither one is correct. However, the debate should have some merits to what is being said. Some things that exist in this biography will be opinionated. There are other things that are not debate-able. They are facts through personal experiences, creditable information, books, and news media. All of these sources of information can be deemed as factual. Only personal opinions can be disagreed with. We all have our opinions on certain issues, but those opinions do not make us totally correct on them.

Progressive Presidential Race: as the race continues, it becomes more interesting each day. I have learned much about how we elect our Public officials. I have seen just how far the candidates will go in trying to get elected. The smear and lies that is told in trying to persuade the public's opinion of one another. Hate mail, threats of violence, conspiring to demean one another. I know that this is the way that it has been done for decades if not centuries. This is something that I cannot agree with in our society. We accept this way of campaigning. The candidates should present the very best out of our society. It seems if though we condone this type of campaigning. Down and dirty, say any thing, do any things type of politics. Debates should be on the true issues, true statements and a symbol of what a society should be like. Candidates should be setting the examples of what and how they want their citizens to be like. The whole of society is watching and listening to how these candidates present themselves and their agendas. If we want an un-corrupt and honorable society, then our candidates should present themselves in that way, our way of living and carrying on in our society hinges on how our leaders will lead our people. Many in our society feed on negativity, they like to see and hear negative things that is said and done. Many of these people say that they are Christians; this is an insult to the meaning of our Christian faith. These people are a long ways from being Christ like. This is hypocritical in it self, professing to be something that you are not. For many decades, we have accepted this type of hypocritical indulgence. Strict guide lines should be set for candidates to follow. When they stray away from these guide lines then they should be penalized for those actions. This is one way of taking the lies and corruption out of campaigning. Our society should not expect anything less than honorable, and credibility in our officials. This is the first time that I have spent so much time in watching television on the candidates and their policies, I have seen how they try to break their opponents down, how they want to degrade them and even attack their religious affiliations. The negativity seems to be the order of the day. Many of us feed on this negativity and the candidates say what they think that the public wants to hear. The hope is that we will put an end to this kind of campaigning. It is the people that will set a new course of what is not allowed in our officials in seeking our public office. We have the power to make a change.

We are on the verge of selecting the very first Black, President in our nation's history, the young man of mixed races has come farther in this race than any other Black or racially mixed person has ever been in this most important position in our society. This young man is very intelligent, spiritual and he has good judgments in making decisions. The only thing that would keep him from being elected as the first Black President would be racism. There would be no other reason for him not to be elected for this office but the hatred and racism in our society. No one ever thought that he would have come this far in his pursuit of the highest office in the nation. The young man looks and acts the part of being a leader. He has the right spirit that guides him, the right people that are about him and supports his candidacy. With God being in his corner, and the right people supporting him, he is on his way to farther make history. There have been many obstacles tossed in his way; lies, smear, and plain old racism have been in his path to the oval office. If God be with you, then there is nothing that the devil can do to stop him. For us that want change in a more positive direction for our country, we should pray for him to succeed in achieving this goal. Our country, our world, our society and our community needs a change from the direction in which we are traveling. He will be a better representative for our country to the rest of the world for our people. He has the good judgments and the intelligence of communicating with other countries of the world. The old ways of doing business should be eliminated. The future should be embraced, with new ideas, new people, and seeking of peace instead of war. This will be the answer to our problems. We should be able to sit down with others that disagree with us and have a true dialogue. We are no longer a country unto our selves, we are a world's community and we all working together to solve the world's problems. The world has become smaller. Through communication, transportation we have maximized our associations with other nations of the world. This approach will make it better for all. For many years, this was only a hope and a dream for many, through hard work, it is now a reality.

We now have three days to go, and then we will have the Presidential election. To this point, the election has gone back and forth. The democratic nominee has for a long time held his lead, the margin between the two candidates have been seven to eight points in the national polls apart from each other. The republican nominee has thrown everything that he could throw at him to stop his momentum. The democratic nominee kept focused on his goal, he refused to get caught up in all the lies, smears and deception that plagued this campaign from the off set. The sights were set high and kept moving his candidacy forward, never letting the obstacles stop his momentum. He is a man with a mission, and the mission is to the White House. Nearly everything that he has done was historical. He had the largest crowds to come to his campaigns, he has raised more money than any other candidate in the history of campaigning, and he is the first Black that ever comes this far in the race for the White House. All of his speeches have been historical. None of this could have been possible, if it had not been for the people that blazed the trail before him. He was a knowledgeable candidate. He had high marks in one of the most prestigious schools in the nation. He earned respect from the students and the administrators of that school. He also was respected in his Chicago's neighborhood. He had seen the need of the people there and he wanted to do something to make their lives a little bit better. He had witnessed all the things that would demoralize the community. He is truly the right man at the right time for the right job. The nation need to be changed, there has been for too long, during business as usual. It is a new and young man in town; he is for all the people, not for a hand full of the wealthiest. This is my endorsement for his pursuit of the oval office. He has everything going his way, he have much of the nation is behind him. He has millions that financially supports his candidacy. And the most important of all, God is with him. So how can he lose? This is what the country is crying for, a God sent representative of the nation.

We should remember that nothing happens when we want it to happen, but when God is in the plan he will act when he see fit to act. Those that went before him never saw the results of their prayers and their labors, but the seed had been planted for others to see it grow. The seed was planted on good fertile ground and the suffering and prayers of those people was the fertilizer to make the dream grow. It is now at a fast paced growing cycle and nothing can turn the growth around. Keeping good fertilizer on and around the plant will mature into a blooming plant. We all will benefit from the hard work of those that went before us, those that plowed the fields and knocked down obstacles that were in the way of progress. We all have a hand in growing this plant. During what we know is the right thing to do. And to those that want a more positive change in our society and in our world. He has not been elected yet, but if we continue to work for change and continue to pray for a better nation, and the world, we will have a better place for all to live. Hunger could be minimized; greed could be at a minimum, our environment. We need someone to want to preserve this world of ours, we should all be good stewards of our plant and lead the world in having a safe environment, and by showing the other nations of the world how we should preserve our planet. We need a communicator, someone that can, and willing to sit down and talk to leaders of other nations in trying to resolve some of the problems that face our world, a leader that won't look down on other leaders of the world. Sharing the resources and power over our planet, there is no doubt that unification is better than division. For too long, our leaders have tried to classify us and keep individuals, nations, groups, races, rich and poor divided and separated from each other. This will be a hard job for the next President of our country; the hole has been dug deep and will get deeper until someone stops the digging. We are on our way to electing an intelligent leader that will plot a new course for us to take. People are ready for something different, something new, a different direction.

The Long Journey

Two days before the presidential election; the race is heating up more than ever, at this stage of the election, every thing seem to be fair game for the candidates. They will use any thing or any means to hold their position in the running, or do anything to gain the lead for presidential advantages. At this point in the running, no one know who will win the election, the running has been close and the public is un-certain on who they will vote for in these last days of campaigning. Those who will vote for their own respective candidate, their minds have been made up early in the running. For those that are looking for a reason not to vote, are the ones that are looking for an excuse not to vote for the other candidate. There are many excuses why they have not made a decision on the particular candidate. We cannot deny that racism is one of the main reasons, some will not admit it but it does exist. The excuses are: he is too young, he is too inexperienced, he is too Black; he is a Muslim, and a terrorist. He has been labeled as a socialist and any thing else that they could throw in his pass. The democratic candidate has remained steady, his eyes is on the most important things in our society. With two days to go before the election, he has retained a lead. So far, all of the negativity that the other side has thrown at him, he has withstood it. He has all of his supporters working hard for him to retain his position and do not be swayed from the course that he is now on. The truth will triumph out all of the negativity that has been put in his way. God is, and God will be for the young man until the end of his mission. This is the only way that our society and our world can go forward. There have to be a changing of the guards, someone with a different vision, a different kind of a politics. If we choose not to elect the young man, that have made history in nearly all categories and put another man in the white house with the same views of the last presidency, then they will have to accept what ever they buy. The choices are very clear to the clear thinking public, make a change, or experience most of the same. The "same" has been mostly negative. This race is not a race to base all upon experience, it is "experience" that has the country in the predicament that we are now. They have tried many different ways of de-railing his candidacy, but they were not successful. He kept on his game plan to reach the White House. I am following his journey to the White House.

Final chapter on my "journey" For two years I have been watching the campaigning of each of the candidates, during this time, I have seen and heard much negativity in the race democratic nominee would not be denied. He won the election on this historical date: November 4th, 20008 the first black or none White person to ever be elected for the nation's highest office. I have been blessed to be alive to see this historical moment in my life. My journey started many years ago, I have seen many things and heard much more, but this is the biggest historical event that I have witnessed. I wonder what all of the "trail blazers" that had gone before him would say, if they could have witnessed this historical event. My parents never would have dreamed of having a Black president in their near future. Mother did not live to see it happen, she died five years earlier. This is a true testament that things in our society are changing. The young people will be the ones that will make this change. They have seen what the older leaders of our country have done to us and nations of the world, now it is time for change. No longer can the old leaders teach the young, would be leaders of our nation to do business as usual. The young people know where the true problems exist. We all should get behind our newly elected President and help him and his cabinet to turn our country around. The older leaders want things to remain as they always been. They don't really want change. The first thing that they are concerned about is their wealth and how they are going to keep it. These are the greedy people in our society that keeps the business as usual mentality. These are the final words on my journey through life. I have been blessed to see a changing of the leadership. I have seen the first Black Presidential elect in our history. I have seen history made on nearly ever front for the race for the white house. Perhaps in the future, color of a man's skin will not be a major concern in determining who is better to represent us in public office. The credibility, character knowledge and the contents of a person's heart should be the criteria for selecting a person for a position. In selecting this candidate, the Hands of God was in the plan. Our country was at one of the lowest points in our history. People were losing their retirement benefits, their homes, their jobs and we have two wars going on. There were mistrust in our government, our energy consumption had risen to an all time high, and gasoline for our vehicles that we use to travel back and forth to work in had gotten out of control, our food consumption at an all time high. All of these things were put before the citizens to deal with. Frustrations were growing at an alarming rate. People were ready for a change in our government. This would not have been possible without these obstacles that were bringing us to our knees. The young candidate came to front at the right time, he had a different agenda. He was bright and well schooled on our needs and offered a solution to the problems that faced our nation. The hard, hearted and racist elements of our society had to be brought to their lowest point in their life to be ready for any one that would offer them a relief from the dwindling economy. It took the Hand of a more superior power to melt the hearts of these hard, hearted people. Their hearts had not melted down and their minds had not been changed, this selection of the right candidate at the right time would not be possible. People had begun to think that man can change if he is forced to change. Change did not come from them acting alone, there were forces that were impose upon them to have a change of heart. A candidate that was a spiritual, God trusting and believing individual, this could perhaps, be one of the greatest stories that was ever told in modern times, up from the ashes, and becoming the most important person in the modern world or perhaps in the world as a whole. He would have influence over much of the world, and he would be looked upon to solve most of the world's problems. He is on a mission, sent by God almighty. Whosoever God places in a position of power, there is no man that can remove him from this appointment, if we want change in our society and in our world, we all should back him and pray for him to be successful in this position. History has been made through out his campaign. Let us help him, our Nation and our World.

Recognition of the" Trail Blazers," none of this could have been possible, if the trail to the presidency had not been blazed by these heroic fore- runners. Those people gave everything that they had to see a day such as this. Some were jailed, beaten, murdered and deceived in every way to de-rail them from this course of pursuit for equality, justice and the pursuit of the American dream. These people had blazed a clear trail for those that would follow. We have not yet reached our destination, but much progress has been made. Many of these blazers have fallen along the way side, but the March and pursuit continues. We all have a role to play on this trail to justice, equality and our pursuit to happiness and to a better world. It all starts at home, in our own back yard. Then we can show the rest of the world how it is done. For many decades, we have told the world how they should live, what they should do and how they should act on the world's stage. For decades, we have lived in opposite of what we have been teaching others to do. It is now time to step up to the plate and live the way that we have encouraged others to live. This is truly a time of truth. We either" put up or we should shut up on telling others what to do". For those fore- runners, the seeds that they had planted will not be in vain. Many never saw the plants grow but to those who did, they know that faith, constant prayer and much suffering had produced many results. Let us all continue on the trail that have already been blazed by our fore -runners. The distance is long and we have new blazers coming aboard at any given time. Pass the baton and stay on the trail.

Through all off the campaigning, hard work, resistant lays deceit, fabricating, insults, threats, and racism and other evil doings. The people that had worked hard on the President's elect behalf now can rest a little easier. The hard fight has been won. Thanks to all of those dedicated people who never ceased to quit working hard for his campaign. The will of the people have spoken. History is now extending it pages. I have no doubt that he is the right man for the job. All of his supporters deserve a tremendous applause for the work that they had done in getting him to become the historically, first Black/White President in American History. He is the first of any race, other than a White male. This is a true indication of this being a new time and a more informed new and younger generation. These new Americans are ready for a change. None of this could have been possible without God's hand there to guide them through. All the thanks and all of the praise go to someone that is not of this world, but he is here to watch over and to steer us in the right direction. Let us all pray for him and stand behind him in trying to lead this country in the right direction. If God is with him and our country then there is nothing that can or will turn us around. I have been blessed to see this historical moment, now I am waiting for the Historical Inauguration of the first Black/White, President of our United States of America. This is our Country, January he will be inaugurated into the White House. Record numbers of people will travel to the District of Columbia, It have been estimated that millions will be there for his inauguration. This is a time for people around the world to become part of History, being made here in our Country. This should change many hearts and minds, now the rest off the world can see the best things that our Country has to offer. We are a Country that can adapt to change and reality. The good wills eventually, over-take the evils of our Nation and our World. Let us help in making this change. Although my personal journey is coming to a close, the Nation's journey must continue. It is good to close out the journey through my life with the inauguration of our first Black/White, President in American History and in the Western World. The last pages will be written when he is inaugurated and officially, become the first White/Black to hold the Presidential seat; January 2009 this will become a reality and Historical. This event is so important that it is worth waiting until this time. When it happens, then I will finish my last comments on such a Historical undertaking.

Route to the White House: from Philadelphia to Washington D.C., is a Historical Route that was used by Abraham Lincoln. This route come across the mason Dixon line and is a concern for the security off the President Elect and his family, there are many overpasses and bridges that he will come under and over to reach Washington D.C., there are still people out there that harbors hate in their hearts, they would think of nothing that would stop them from trying to sabotage the train or try spoil the trip to the White House. This is a historical train trip and the security is at an all time high. There are few stops along the way, but the train will be traveling at a very low speed, greeting people along the route. Coming into Wilmington, Delaware to pick up his Vice President, and from there into Baltimore, where he will give a speech, and from there, into Washington D.C., this is where he will be inaugurated for our next President. There were four speeches given along the route to Washington D.C., he spoke in Philadelphia, Edge Wood, Baltimore and in Washington D.C., here he will await his inauguration into the White House and his Presidency. The route was Historical and the places that he spoke at were off Historical significance. This was the same route that Mr. Lincoln took to become inaugurated. There are record crowds where ever he traveled small towns, along the highways, people greeting the train and all off his followers. I believe that this man is on a mission, and the mission is sent by God. None can deny this.

There is no other man that is alive today that could have such an impact with people off all Races, Nations, Religions and classifications. Even the hardest off the heart- hearted had seen the light. Only God could have made this dream come true. People came together under a single cause. Change was the theme of his campaign. A new and different direction of how the Country should go. Bringing people together and trying to unify the Country as a whole was his success to the White House. Now let us all do our Part and try to help him, carry-out his mission of change and a new direction. This is January 2009, and three days left for him to become the only person in our History, other than a White male to hold the President position in the United States of America. When he is sworn in as our next President then the writing of this portion of my journey conclude, the journey of the Nation will continue and the way is made even clearer. This is Sunday, January 2009. The celebration and honor continued. Celebrities had dedicated their talents to his honor. Hundreds off thousands spectators, well wishers, supporters from around the world attended this recognition of him being the next President. Even those who did not vote for him attended the celebration. Minds had been changed among those who were un-decided. There was something about him that would draw people to him. His smiles and his sincerity could be seen by those who supported him, and by those who opposed him. There was no fault found in him for this office. There were many who tried to derail him along the way, but the masses of people had spoken. God was in this plan and no man or groups off men can change what God had placed in their hearts and minds.

The Long Journey

Pre-inauguration goes on; Sunday night, celebrities had parties and social gatherings in his honor. Celebrities from all over the Country took part in celebrations. People had hope and they believed he was the one that would help make this a reality. Monday, he went to schools and other public places in the D.C., area and socialized with the citizens of the city. He talked with students and teachers concerning their needs, he wanted to show that he was interested in their concerns. His presence was well received. This is Martin Luther King's anniversary date: January 19, and all of these events seem to come together. King's dream seem to have come true, although he is not around to see it happen, his seeds had been planted and now they are catching root. All of the supporters that marched with King are proud to see this day. A party was given for his opponent, the one that he defeats in the Republican Party for the Presidential seat. Honor was given to his opponent for the services that he had given to our Country. January 2009, President Elect, is now the Official President of these United States of America, he was sworn in by the Chief Justice. We now have the first Black/white, President in our American History.

This truly was a Historical time in the making. Generations to come can look back in this time in History and cherish this moment. I have waited for the official swearing in off the President, before I would conclude this portion of "the long journey", long journey and the journey of our Nation will continue, we as a nation have many miles to travel before our journey is complete. Let us all do our part in trying to reach the destination, when one falls down then others will lift them up. Nation's journey will continue until we all reach our destination as a people. Help the new President in every way that we can, to make this a success for all off our people. One part of the journey ends, but another will began. May God Bless Him and our Nation? Let us all pray for our world to have peace, and prosperity for other nations of the world. Together, we can!

Why did I want to write this journal and what motivated me to write about my long journey through life? There are several reasons for me to want to write about my long journey. I had an urge to write something that pertain to my life and my surroundings my parents and my friends who were an important part off my life, my grandparents, uncles and aunts. All off my cousins. These people will never be forgotten. After reading books and learning about the authors and their lives and their many encounters in walking their journey, this was what I had wanted to do for many years before I decided to just do it. I had the information stored within me to release to others, I wanted others to feel what I feel and to just think on the same line of thoughts that I was thinking on. It was like a balloon that was full of air and ready to explode if I did not release some of the air that is within it. The difference is, I had information that I wanted to share with others. It took me late into my life to try to tell my story to the best of my ability. All events that is in my journal is factual, either through experience, creditable information from my love ones and friends, and the feelings that I have in trying to relay the information that I have stored inside of me. When I was a young boy in school, reading books, such as" Wink and wink" it motivated me to want to express myself through writing. This book was a good book for grade school students to read. This built a foundation for me to want to continue my urge for more and better reading of the obstacles in life's journey.

There were too many people leaving the earth that I knew, and little was known about their history or their parent's history. Most Black people can only go back four generations, we can remember our grand parents if we are fortunate to do so, few can remember their Great grand parents. Our parents do not know much or anything at all about their grand parents. There should be a hunger for us to try to find out more about our ancient ancestors. If it was possible that we were able to talk to them about their life's struggle, we would be saddened, things that they had to endure just to remain alive. This is the information that I seek, those old people are gone and cannot tell their stories, but we that are left alive should try to tell as much about their life as possible. I wanted to tell what I have heard, lived, and experienced in my journey. I want others to know what I think about the world's situation, our nation's problems and how we arrived to this level in our lives.

Now that I have gathered more knowledge and understanding on how to put my thoughts and experiences in writing, I feel like I have been vindicated. We all have a story to tell, but no one else will ever know of it until it is put into writing. All of the past generations had a story tell, if only they could have read and write their story, if only they were allowed to try to express their thoughts, visions and dreams, if laws were not on the books to prohibit them from learning to read and write their stories. Although there were forces against them, they tried to relay their stories to us in the best way that they could. Their stories will be carried out through us. This journal will tell of some of the thoughts and dreams that they had for us.

These are the reasons why my urge to try to write about my feelings and the creditable information of some off the older parents. We all owe much to those older ancestors; they endured the hard ship of life, so our generation could become more free and knowledgeable about the world that we lived in. Their suffering paved the way for us progress and see their dreams come true p from the ashes of the earth, to the more powerful positions in our nation and in the world. This was their dreams. Few off them lived to see their dreams come true. This is why I was motivated to try to tell my story.

Mother and foster grandson—Flora Bryant and Thomas Horseman.

My father, James Bryant Senior.

James and Mae, husband and wife, standing together.

James and his brother Eli, standing together.

This is the photo of Samuel and his lovely wife, Judy Bryant

The elder daughter of James and Mae Bryant

Joyce Marie and her daughter, Rhea Mae

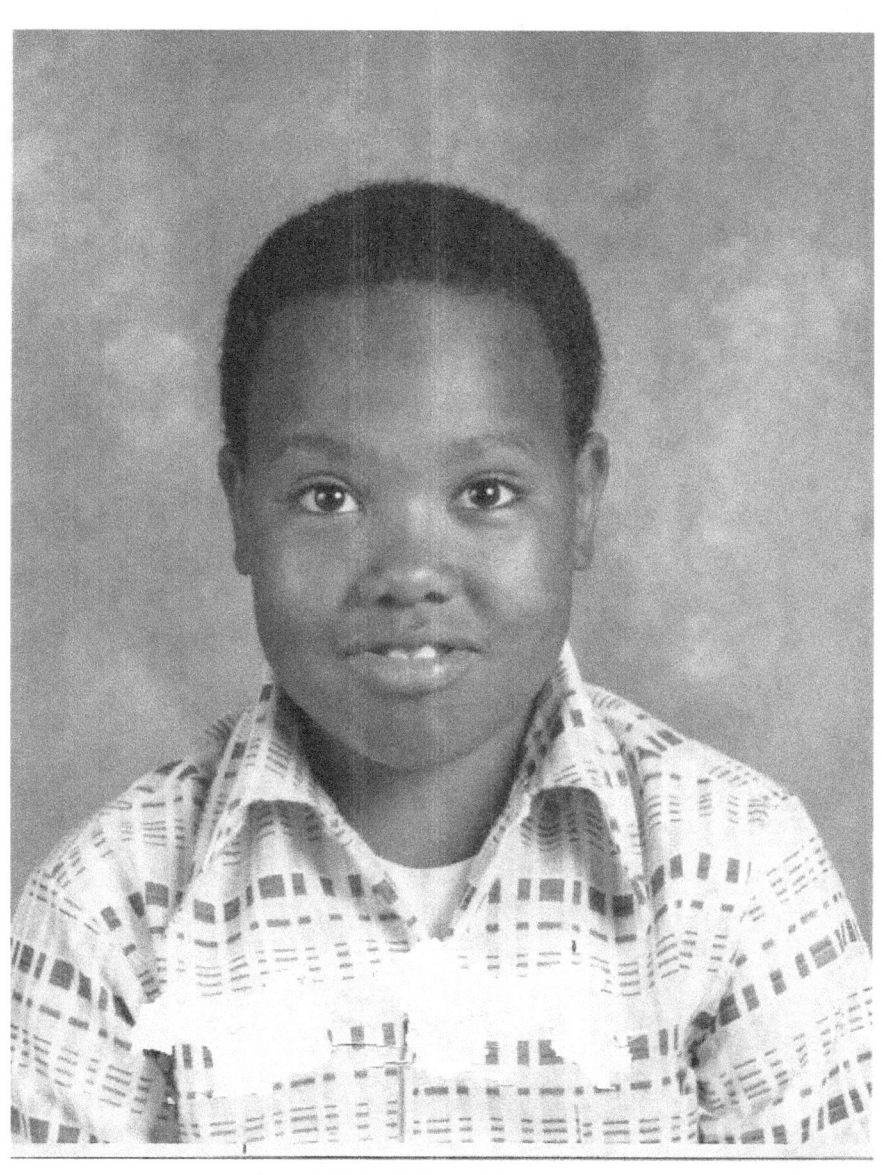

Michael Darrel Bryant

Carla Marie Bryant

Lauren Whitney Forbes

Sister Florene and her husband, Arthur Spires

Reyanna, granddaughter of James and Mae Bryant

Kaya, the great-granddaughter of James and Mae Bryant

Isaiah, the great-grandson of James and Mae Bryant

Thomas, a son and right-hand man in our family and loved by all

www.ingramcontent.com/pod-product-compliance
Lightning Source LLC
Chambersburg PA
CBHW071613080526
44588CB00010B/1115